Pathway

Comprehension

Reading • Listening • Viewing

Einführungsphase
Sekundarstufe II

Herausgegeben von:
Iris Edelbrock

Erarbeitet von:
Waltraud Feger, Julia Rüttgers,
Karola Schallhorn, Jessica Vogel

Sprachliche Betreuung:
Ronnie Halligan

Schöningh

Die Begleitmaterialien zu „Pathway“ können über den Buchhandel oder direkt beim Verlag bezogen werden:

- **Students' Book**
  Best.-Nr. 040175
- **Audio-CDs**
  Hörtexte und Songs
  Best.-Nr. 062531
- **Grammar and Skills Trainer**
  Best.-Nr. 040176
- **Differenzierungsmaterial**
  Best.-Nr. 040177

Weitere Informationen finden Sie unter www.schoeningh-schulbuch.de.

www.schoeningh-schulbuch.de
Schöningh Verlag, Jühenplatz 1–3, 33098 Paderborn

Druck A 5 4 3 2 1 / Jahr 2019 18 17 16 15
Alle Drucke der Serie A sind im Unterricht parallel verwendbar.
Die letzte Zahl bezeichnet das Jahr dieses Druckes.

Illustrationen: Matthias Berghahn, Bielefeld
Umschlaggestaltung: Nora Krull, Bielefeld; Fotos: © Frans Lemmens/Corbis und © Oote Boe/OKAPIA
Druck und Bindung: westermann druck GmbH, Braunschweig

ISBN 978-3-14-040168-5

Contents

Common Grounds and Cultural Clashes?! – Living Together in the 21st Century

The Global Village – The World in a Nutshell?!

Virtual Communities and Social Networks – Living in the Digital Age

All texts for reading comprehension can be found in the Students' Book (Bestell-Nr. 040175).

The material for listening comprehension can be found on the Audio-CDs (Bestell-Nr. 062531).

The material for viewing comprehension can be found on the CD-ROM in the inside back cover of the Students' Book (Bestell-Nr. 040175).

Vorwort

Liebe Kollegin, lieber Kollege,

das vorliegende Comprehension-Material stellt Ihnen die neuen, **in den Kernlehrplänen geforderten standardisierten Aufgabenformate** für die **Kompetenzen**

- *Reading Comprehension*
- *Listening Comprehension*
- *Audio-visual Comprehension*

zur Verfügung.

Die **offenen, halboffenen und geschlossenen Aufgabenformate** folgen der Chronologie der Units und der Materialien des Schülerbuches und können sowohl zur **Leistungsüberprüfung** wie auch als das Schülerbuch **ergänzende und differenzierende Materialien** im Unterricht oder zur häuslichen Bearbeitung eingesetzt werden.

Bei inhaltlich oder sprachlich komplexen Materialien des Schülerbuches werden i. d. R. mehrere unterschiedliche Aufgabenformate angeboten, die weitere Lern- und Arbeitsschritte (*scaffolding*) ermöglichen oder überprüfen. Sie unterstützen damit

- das **Globalverstehen** von Texten
- **selektives Verstehen** von Texten (z. B. das Ermitteln von leicht lokalisierbaren Informationen)
- das **Detailverstehen** (Ermittlung von Einzelinformationen unter Beachtung eines Beziehungsgefüges)
- **interferierendes Verstehen** (Ermitteln von Informationen, die aus dem Text geschlussfolgert werden müssen).

Mögliche Aufgabenformate:

- *multiple choice* (mit und ohne Textbeleg; eine/mehr als eine korrekte Antwort)
- *true-false (-not given)* (mit Textbeleg)
- *sentence/text completion* (Ergänzungsaufgaben)
- *sequencing* (richtige Reihenfolge herstellen)
- *note taking/mapping information*
- *short answers*
- *gapped summary*
- *correcting mistakes*
- *identifying grammatical phenomena*
- *citing/giving evidence from the text*

"My reading comprehension is so-so, but I make up for it with my highlighting skills."

Darüber hinaus bietet Ihnen das Material zahlreiche ***follow-up activities***, die an die Hör- und Leseverstehensübungen anknüpfen und damit auch die Anforderungsbereiche II (*analysis*) und III (*comment/evaluation*) einbeziehen und im unmittelbaren Zusammenhang mit den Texten und Aufgabenapparaten des Schülerbuches stehen.

Jedes Aufgabenmaterial ist mit **umfangreichen Lösungen** versehen, die ebenfalls der **unterrichtlichen Differenzierung** und **individuellen Förderung** von Schülern dienen können.

Ihr Pathway Team

Audio CD 1, Track 1

1 Sting
Tomorrow We'll See – Introductory Remarks

Sting, whose real name is Gordon Matthew Thomas Sumner, born near Newcastle in 1951, is one of the most talented and successful singers in the world. He has written almost 300 songs (music and lyrics) and masters several instruments and is also known as a film actor.

a) Listen to Sting's song 'Tomorrow We'll See'. While listening twice, make notes on the following topics:

> **to shed** to get rid of sth. that is no longer wanted; *loswerden* – **tawdry** *billig und geschmacklos* – **luster** *Schimmer* – **tights** *Seidenstrümpfe* – **to run** here: *Laufmaschen haben* – **headlights** *Scheinwerfer* – **to judge sb./sth.** to form an opinion about sb./sth.; *jdn./etw. beurteilen* – **to wind (wound, wound) up as** *(phr.v., infml.)* to find yourself in a particular place or situation; *werden, enden als* – **to stain** *beflecken* – **next of kin** *(idm.)* your closest living relative(s) – **abode** *(fml.)* the place where sb. lives; *Bleibe, Wohnsitz*

1. the setting ______________________________

____

2. the singer on his outward appearance ______________________________

____

3. his body language ______________________________

____

____

4. dealing with his customers ______________________________

____

____

5. his friend ______________________________

____

____

6. his customers ______________________________

____

7. his future ______________________________

____

____

8. the meaning of the refrain ______________________________

____

____

b) After the third listening, try to complete the beginnings to the following sentences:

1. The topic of the song is/deals with ______________________________

____

2. The singer represents ______________________________

____

3. His life is ______________________________

____

4. His customers are ______________________________

____

____

5. He remembers his friend, who ______________________________

____

____

6. The singer's problems turn out to be ______________________________

____

____

7. In the refrain, the singer asks the listener ______________________________

____

____

c) Imagine you want to make your friend listen to Sting's song on youtube, but your friend wants you to give him/her some kind of a summary first. What would you tell him/her?

____

____

____

____

____

____

d) Now listen to Sting's introduction to the song sung at a live concert in Berlin in 2010.

coherent logical and well-organized – **narrative,** *(n., fml.)* story – **muse** inspiration – **to merge from sth.** to come out of a hidden place – **transsexual** a person who feels that he/she wants to live, dress etc. as a member of the opposite sex; esp. one who has a medical operation to change his/her sexual organs – **realm** an area of interest or knowledge, *Bereich, Gebiet* – **subconscious** *(n.) Unterbewusstsein* – **insistent** *beharrlich, hartnäckig* – **judgmental** *wertend, voreingenommen* – **to dare sth.** *etw. wagen* – **Roxanne** a song written by Sting, released in 1978, written from the point of view of a man who falls in love with a prostitute – **confidence** a feeling of trust – **inch** a unit for measuring length; equal to 2.54 cm – **heel** *Absatz*

After the second listening, give a short answer to the following questions:

1. How did Sting go about creating this song?

2. What was his problem?

After a third listening to Sting's remarks, apply them to the song and answer the following questions.

3. What is his message?

4. When Sting mentioned 'a male transsexual prostitute' the audience laughed openly. What do you think may have been the reasons?

Follow-up activity

e) Find the correct adverbs to comment on the information in the following sentences: Example: My friend was murdered. (I am really sorry about it.)
Sadly, my friend was murdered.
Choose the right one from the box:

typically • obviously • unwisely • luckily • coincidentally • unfortunately • honestly • worryingly • thankfully • fortunately • happily • obviously • certainly

1. I wanted to go to Sting's concert in London. (That goes without saying.)

____

2. I did not have enough money for the ticket. (That is the truth.)

____

3. My parents had forbidden me to go to any concert. (That was quite typical of them.)

____

4. I had told them about my bad mark in maths. (It was a bad decision.)

____

5. (I was very lucky,) my grandmother helped me to get their permission.

____

6. My grandma is a fan of Sting herself and gave me some extra pocket money. (That goes without saying.)

____

7. But I was late for the ticket office – all the tickets had already been sold. (That was not good at all.)

____

8. At the gate, I met my friend whose brother had not come. (That was mere chance.)

____

____

9. I took his brother's ticket. (I was so happy about that and thanked him.)

____

Audio CD 1, Track 1

1 Sting
Tomorrow We'll See – Introductory Remarks

a) Listen to Sting's song 'Tomorrow We'll See'. While listening twice, make notes on the following topics:

1. the setting: a rainy day on the outskirts of a town, red-light district, meeting point for hustlers/male prostitutes

2. the singer on his outward appearance: skirt too short, heels too high, tights with runs, typical presentation of a prostitute

3. his body language: smoking too much, waiting for costumers (slow night), studying the cars and drivers passing by, he checks, winks, smiles and waves his hand to attract attention

4. dealing with his customers: bargaining with a customer before getting into his car, pleading to get more money from him, has second thoughts on starting "his business"

5. his friend: a relative was murdered while going about the same "business", living on the streets, a tramp and male prostitute, whose body was disposed of, whose place was taken by some body else

6. his customers: are the ones who have money, he has the body to sell to them

7. his future: does not seem bright, he is aware that it is up to him, does not want to make excuses but goes ahead, saying he needs the money to support himself

8. the meaning of the refrain: pleading with his audience not to condemn him, the same fate could befall anybody, wants to go on "one more night", if he strikes it lucky, there may be a change in his life the next day

b) After the third listening, try to complete the beginnings to the following sentences:

1. The topic of the song is the sad life of a male prostitute. The song deals with the singer's reflections on his life in the red-light district.

2. The singer represents an outcast of society/a transsexual on the outskirts of a town trying "to make a living".

3. His life is bleak, as he has no prospect of a bright/better future.

4. His customers are of mixed intentions, pay him for sex, may lead a double life, like John (in his other life), representing double moral standards.

5. He remembers his friend, who was also his relative, whom he pities because he was murdered and then disposed of, leaving no gap as someone else took his place on the street/is maybe aware that he risks experiencing the same fate.

6. The singer's problems turn out to be manifold: lack of money/no proper job/perhaps having dropped out of school/totally dependent on selling his body/risky life

7. In the refrain, the singer asks the listener not to condemn his way of making a living. He pleads with him not to judge him prematurely as the listener himself/herself might run into the same difficulties in another life. He seems positive about bringing about a change in his life, maybe the very next day.

c) Imagine you want to make your friend listen to Sting's song on youtube, but your friend wants you to give him/her some kind of a summary first. What would you tell him/her?

The tune is rather sad and suits the lyrics well.

The story being told by a singer, who is a male prostitute waiting for customers in a red-light district, deals with thoughts on his own way of life and memories of a relative and friend, who was a tramp and prostitute like himself and was murdered. The refrain underlines the singer's/composer's intention to blow a breach for social outcasts. The song is not totally pessimistic since the speaker/singer has some hope of changing his way of life as one can recognize in the line: 'Tomorrow we'll see'. These words are, however, not very convincing.

d) Now listen to Sting's introduction to the song sung at a live concert in Berlin in 2010.
After the second listening, give a short answer to the following questions:

1. How did Sting go about creating this song? The creation of the music and lyrics did not happen simultaneously. The music was composed first and the composer was then at a loss to find the adequate text matching his tune.

2. What was his problem?

His muse/inspiration surprised him with the idea of devoting this song to a transsexual prostitute. He is then aware that he does not know much about this field/sphere and wants to give up the idea. But when he is reminded of his other song 'Roxanne', he makes up his mind to carry on with his first idea and pay heed to the voice coming from his subconscious. He makes up his mind that – as an artist – he has to assume the role of this outcast and face the world from his position and attitude.

After a third listening to Sting's remarks, apply them to the song and answer the following questions:

3. What is his message?

As the refrain repeats several times, people should not judge or condemn those who are living outside the common standard, as many are simply hiding away some dark side of their existence and we, in a different world, could be in their position. Sting – as an artist – feels it to be his duty to open the listener's eyes and blow a breach for the outcasts.

4. When Sting mentioned 'a male transsexual prostitute' the audience laughed openly. What do you think may have been the reasons?

With his song 'Roxanne' on their minds, maybe they thought that another libertine song was imminent. When they laughed a second time (after "my experience of the realm is zero"), it was laughter of disbelief as Sting had acted in the role of a bisexual butler and the scene could be watched on youtube.

Follow up activity

e) Find the correct adverbs to comment on the information in the following sentences: Choose the right one from the box:

1. I wanted to go to Sting's concert in London. (That goes without saying.)

Obviously/Naturally/Certainly, I wanted to go to Sting's concert.

2. I did not have enough money for the ticket. (That is the truth.)

I honestly did not have enough money for the ticket.

3. My parents had forbidden me to go to any concert. (That was quite typical of them.)

Typically, my parents had forbidden me to go to any concert.

4. I had told them about my bad mark in maths. (It was a bad decision.)

I had told them unwisely about my bad mark in maths.

5. (I was very lucky,) my grandmother helped me to get their permission.

Luckily/Fortunately, my grandmother helped me to get their permission.

6. My grandma is a fan of Sting herself and gave me some extra pocket money. (That goes without saying.)

Obviously, my grandma is a fan of Sting herself and gave me some extra money.

7. But I was late for the ticket office – all the tickets had already been sold. (That was not good at all.)

But I was late for the ticket office – unfortunately, all the tickets had already been sold.

8. At the gate, I met my friend whose brother had not come. (That was mere chance.)

Unexpectedly/Coincidentally, I met my friend, whose brother had not come.

I unexpectedly met my friend whose brother had not come.

9. I took his brother's ticket. (I was so happy about that and thanked him.)

I thankfully/happily took his brother's ticket.

Students' Book, pp. 14 ff.

2 Joel Stein
The Me Me Me Generation

This magazine article, taken from TIME, deals with the attempt to find out about the generation that was born between 1980 and 2000, the so called Millennials, who – apart from a few positive characteristics – seem to be lazy, fame-obsessed and self-centered – in comparison to earlier generations – and have developed narcissistic personalities as they are addicted to materialism, social media and technology.

a) Read the text and then check the statements below. If the statement is wrong, make corrections in note form. Note down the lines you refer to in order to prove whether the statement is right or wrong. You have 45 minutes for the task. One example is given.

		True	False
	Millennials got so many participation trophies growing up that a recent study showed that 40 % believe they should be promoted every three years, regardless of performance. *every **two** years*		X (ll. 21–25)
1.	In 1992, the nonprofit Families and Work Institute reported 80 % of people under 23 wanted to one day have a job with greater responsibility; 10 years later, only 60 % did.		
2.	Millennials consist, depending on whom you ask, of people born from 1975 to 2000.		
3.	Each country's millennials are different, but because of globalization, social media, the exporting of Western culture and the speed of change, millennials worldwide are more similar to one another than to older generations within their nations.		
4.	And these aren't just poor-kid problems: rich millennials have even higher rates of Narcissism, materialism and technology addiction in their ghetto-fabulous lives.		
5.	The Industrial Revolution made individuals far more powerful – they could move from a city, start a business, read and form organizations.		
6.	Peer pressure is anti-intellectual. It is anti-historical. It is pro-eloquence.		
7.	Never before have people been able to grow up and reach age 23 so dominated by peers.		

		True	False
8.	Whenever everyone is telling you about their vacation, parties and promotions, you start to embellish your own life to keep up.		
9.	They are pragmatic idealists, tinkerers more than dreamers, life hackers.		
10.	They don't want constant approval but they post photos from the dressing room as they try on clothes.		
11.	They want new experiences, which are more important to them than material goods.		

Follow-up activity

b) Say briefly what you think about the last sentence ("They love their phones but hate talking on them").

c) The new word "selfie" (a kind of self-portrait photograph, typically taken with a hand-held digital camera or smart phone) has been proposed as the "Word of the Year". Would you agree that it is representative of our society?

Students' Book, pp. 14 ff.

2 Joel Stein
The Me Me Me Generation

a)

		True	False
1.	In 1992, the nonprofit Families and Work Institute reported 80% of people under 23 wanted to one day have a job with greater responsibility; 10 years later, only 60% did.	X (ll. 37–40)	
2.	Millennials consist, depending on whom you ask, of people born from 1975 to 2000. *from* **1980** *to 2000*		X (ll. 41 f.)
3.	Each country's millennials are different, but because of globalization, social media, the exporting of Western culture and the speed of change, millennials worldwide are more similar to one another than to older generations within their nations.	X (ll. 47–51)	
4.	And these aren't just poor-kid problems: rich millennials have even higher rates of Narcissism, materialism and technology addiction in their ghetto-fabulous lives. *just* **rich***-kid problems ...:* **poor** *millennials ...*		X (ll. 55–58)
5.	The Industrial Revolution made individuals far more powerful – they could move from a city, start a business, read and form organizations.	X (ll. 63–65)	
6.	Peer pressure is anti-intellectual. It is anti-historical. It is pro-eloquence. **anti***-eloquence*		X (ll. 80 f.)
7.	Never before have people been able to grow up and reach age 23 so dominated by peers.	X (ll. 82–84)	
8.	Whenever everyone is telling you about their vacation, parties and promotions, you start to embellish your own life to keep up.	X (ll. 96–98)	
9.	They are pragmatic idealists, tinkerers more than dreamers, life hackers.	X (ll. 118 f.)	
10.	They don't want constant approval but they post photos from the dressing room as they try on clothes. *They want constant approval – [but] they post ...*		X (ll. 122–124)
11.	They want new experiences, which are more important to them than material goods.	X (ll. 131–133)	

Follow-up activity

b) Say briefly what you think about the last sentence ("They love their phones but hate talking on them").

Personal opinion: This would not be true for me, because I use my mobile for phoning and texting on a fifty-fifty basis/in equal/like measure.

In general: The majority of my friends prefer texting to phoning. I guess it is because then they can go on listening to their iPod or watching TV.

c) The new word "selfie" has been proposed as the "Word of the Year". Would you agree that it is representative of our society?

At least for my generation. When Mrs. Merkel visited the Robert Jungk-Oberschule on 31 March 2014, she became the selfie-star of the pupils when BILD published the students' selfies. Selfies are frequently uploaded to social networking websites. But not only young people take selfies. There was an uproar in the media when Obama took a funeral-selfie. To my mind, selfies have to do with narcissism and self-adulation, too.

Audio CD 1, Track 2

3 John Irving
Owen Meany – Being Attractive to Girls

Listen to the extract from the famous novel *A Prayer for Owen Meany* by John Irving. The narrator describes his friend Owen.
First read the vocabulary and the tasks given below. After the first listening complete tasks a) and b).
After a second listening fill in a profile for Owen Meany. You need not write complete sentences, note form will do (task c)).

awkward here: difficult to deal with – **grasp** here: understanding of sth. – **to deride** to treat sb. or sth. as ridiculous – **ardent** very enthusiastic – **sinewy** *drahtig* – **whippet** *Windhund* – **lean** thin and fit – **rift** *Spaltkeil* – **wedge** *Keil* – **sawyer** *Sägearbeiter* – **slab** a thick, flat piece of stone – **quarry** *Steinbruch* – **remote** isolated – **pit** a deep hole – **to squint** to partly shut your eyes to keep out bright light

a) Match the following adjectives characterizing Owen Meany. One example is given.

a) shy	**b)** awkward	**c)** grown-up	**d)** detached
i) mature	**f)** muscular	**g)** reserved	**h)** difficult
a + g	b +	c +	d +

b) Decide whether the statements are true or false:

		True	False
1.	Owen was a better driver than the narrator.	X	
2.	The narrator was a better student than Owen.		
3.	Owen was often teased by the narrator because of his smallness.		
4.	Girls giggled when they saw Owen and wanted to run away.		
5.	Owen's physical attractiveness was due to regular weightlifting.		
6.	Owen impressed the narrator with his muscles and strength.		
7.	The narrator was a work-mate of Owen that summer.		
8.	Mr. Meany had lost a finger working as a quarryman.		
9.	Owen's profile was that of a well-nourished (*wohlgenährt*) baby.		
10.	The friends were interested in dating sixteen-year old girls.		

c) Fill in a profile for Owen Meany.

1. Age:

____

2. Appearance:

____

____

____

____

____

____

____

3. Career:

____

____

____

____

____

4. Family:

____

____

5. Relation to the narrator:

____

____

____

____

____

____

____

Audio CD 1, Track 2

3 John Irving
Owen Meany – Being Attractive to Girls

a) Match the following adjectives characterizing Owen Meany. One example is given.

a + g	**b** + h	**c** + i	**d** + f

b) Decide whether the statements are true or false:

		True	False
1.	Owen was a better driver than the narrator.	X	
2.	The narrator was a better student than Owen.		X
3.	Owen was often teased by the narrator because of his smallness.	X	
4.	Girls giggled when they saw Owen and wanted to run away.		X
5.	Owen's physical attractiveness was due to regular weightlifting.		X
6.	Owen impressed the narrator with his muscles and strength.	X	
7.	The narrator was a work-mate of Owen that summer.		X
8.	Mr. Meany had lost a finger working as a quarryman.		X
9.	Owen's profile was that of a well-nourished (*wohlgenährt*) baby.		X
10.	The friends were interested in dating sixteen-year old girls.	X	

c) Fill in a profile for Owen Meany.

1. Age:

sixteen

2. Appearance:

attractive; shy; awkward; looked like someone who had had a lot of experience; small/tiny; in command of himself and of others; he had muscles, fiercely strong, sinewy strength of a whippet; frighteningly lean, very adult muscular development; slight fuzz grew on his upper lip, no other traces of a beard, downy, faint moustache; face, nose and eye-sockets, cheekbones and contours of his jaw were like that of a starving person; his face had a permanent, adult quality.

3. Career:

went to school until he was sixteen years old in summer 1958; joins his father's profession as a quarryman working with granite; after starting as a stonecutter and working in the monument shop he becomes a signalman and then a mine-worker like his father.

4. Family:

only his father is mentioned; a quarryman working with granite; he provides Owen with a job in the quarry.

5. Relation to the narrator:

Owen is the narrator's best friend; have been school-buddies; they have grown up with each other; the narrator used to dominate the relationship, teasing Owen because of his smallness; a change in the relationship occurs when Owen turns 16 and starts working; Owen is suddenly in command of everything; he is physically stronger and more attractive; their interests are still the same: sixteen-year-old girls.

Film CD-ROM, Track 1

4 Diablo Cody
Juno – Breaking the Big News

View the extract from the film. Juno meets Bleeker on the sport field. What does she tell him and how do Steve, the one who always teases Juno, and her best friend Leah react to this scene?
After watching tick the correct statements. There is one example given below.

When Bleeker opens the mailbox a lot of ...

☐ matchboxes
☒ Tic-Tac boxes
☐ toads (*Kröten*) flood out of it.

1. ☐ Bleeker does not know where they have come from.
☐ Bleeker has an idea who the sender could be.
☐ Bleeker is annoyed about the mail.

2. ☐ When Bleeker sees Juno approach him he stops jogging and leaves the track.
☐ When he sees Juno approach him he ignores her.
☐ When he sees Juno approach he falls unconscious.

3. ☐ Juno came to tell him that she wanted to break up their relationship.
☐ Juno came to tell him that she had found someone else.
☐ Juno came to apologize for being such a bitch to him the other day.

4. Juno confesses to Bleeker ...
☐ that she is in love with him.
☐ that she is pregnant.
☐ that she wants to marry him.

5. Bleeker says ...
☐ that he never tried to be "the coolest" guy around.
☐ that he actually tried very hard to be cool.
☐ that Juno was the coolest girl around.

6. Everytime Juno sees Bleeker ...
☐ the blood rushes through her veins.
☐ the baby starts kicking.
☐ she gets heartburn (*Sodbrennen*).

7. When Juno and Bleeker kiss, ...
☐ Steve applauds in sympathy.
☐ Steve shows them his middle finger.
☐ Leah makes a friendly joke approving their relation.

Film CD-ROM, Track 1

4 Diablo Cody
Juno – Breaking the Big News

1. ☐ Bleeker does not know where they have come from.
   ☒ Bleeker has an idea who the sender could be.
   ☐ Bleeker is annoyed about the mail.

2. ☒ When Bleeker sees Juno approach him he stops jogging and leaves the track.
   ☐ When he sees Juno approach him he ignores her.
   ☐ When he sees Juno approach he falls unconscious.

3. ☐ Juno came to tell him that she wanted to break up their relationship.
   ☐ Juno came to tell him that she had found someone else.
   ☒ Juno came to apologize for being such a bitch to him the other day.

4. Juno confesses to Bleeker ...
   ☒ that she is in love with him.
   ☐ that she is pregnant.
   ☐ that she wants to marry him.

5. Bleeker says ...
   ☐ that he never tried to be "the coolest" guy around.
   ☒ that he actually tried very hard to be cool.
   ☐ that Juno was the coolest girl around.

6. Everytime Juno sees Bleeker ...
   ☐ the blood rushes through her veins.
   ☒ the baby starts kicking.
   ☐ she gets heartburn (*Sodbrennen*).

7. When Juno and Bleeker kiss, ...
   ☐ Steve applauds in sympathy.
   ☐ Steve shows them his middle finger.
   ☒ Leah makes a friendly joke approving their relation.

Students' Book, pp. 51f.

5 Jeremy Laurance
Hundreds of Websites Urging Girls to "Starve for Perfection"

The British newspaper article at hand depicts the increasing problem that a growing number of Websites promote anorexia and lure teenage girls into dangerous games of dieting and starving all for the sake of the perfect body.

a) Read the newspaper article from *The Independent* and tick off ☒ the right answer:

1. Websites promoting anorexia and related eating disorders

☐ help young girls to improve their beautiful looks.

☐ ask people to stay thin, promoting diets of 1,000 calories a day.

☐ encourage "starving to perfection", featuring pictures of celebrities.

2. Dr. Emma Bond carried out the review which said that

☐ the sites were luring the youngsters to make them addictive.

☐ there was no evidence of commercial involvement.

☐ the sites were set up by groups or individuals to share their experience on slimming.

b) Tick off ☒ the correct ending of the sentence.
The end of the article (ll. 69–79) deals with

☐ the positive results after therapy.

☐ the beginning of anorexia even before adolescence, affecting 3 per cent of teenagers and students.

☐ the threat posed by the websites to be tackled by education and better policing.

c) Study the following three comments of students and say which one comes closest to the message of the article.

Pat
A lot of people talk about anorexia, but I don't know anybody with this condition. Having read the article, I think these dangerous websites should just be forbidden.

Richard
I was not impressed by the article because I think it's more or less only a girls' problem. To my mind this has nothing to do with the internet websites only. The source of the problem is in the family and the parents of those teenagers should be counselled.

Susan

The problem is well-presented although in each case the girl or boy involved is different. His or her addiction to such websites goes hand in hand with his or her distancing himself/herself from his/her friends. Talking is essential to prevent self-harming and developing a borderline personality disorder.

I think ________ 's comment comes quite close to the writer's message, because ____________________

____

____

____

____

____

____

d) The editorial staff had to choose between the photograph on page 51 and another one presenting a set of scales showing the back of a teenager and a dangerously low weight of 43 kg (approx. 94 pounds). Which of the photos seems to match the article more effectively?

To my mind, both photos ____ because

____

____

____

____

____

____

Students' Book, pp. 51 f.

5 Jeremy Laurance
Hundreds of Websites Urging Girls to "Starve for Perfection"

a) Read the newspaper article from *The Independent* and tick off ☒ the right answer.

1. Websites promoting anorexia and related eating disorders

☐ help young girls to improve their beautiful looks.

☐ ask people to stay thin, promoting diets of 1,000 calories a day.

☒ encourage "starving to perfection", featuring pictures of celebrities.

2. Dr. Emma Bond carried out the review which said that

☐ the sites were luring the youngsters to make them addictive.

☒ there was no evidence of commercial involvement.

☐ the sites were set up by groups or individuals to share their experience on slimming.

b) Tick off ☒ the correct ending of the sentence.

☐ The end of the article (ll. 69–79) deals with

☐ the positive results after therapy.

☐ the beginning of anorexia even before adolescence, affecting 3 per cent of teenagers and students.

☒ the threat posed by the websites to be tackled by education and better policing.

c) Study the following three comments of students and say which one comes closest to the message of the article.

Pat
A lot of people talk about anorexia, but I don't know anybody with this condition. Having read the article, I think these dangerous websites should just be forbidden.

Richard
I was not impressed by the article because I think it's more or less only a girls' problem. To my mind this has nothing to do with the internet websites only. The source of the problem is in the family and the parents of those teenagers should be counselled.

Susan
The problem is well-presented although in each case the girl or boy involved is different. His or her addiction to such websites goes hand in hand with his or her distancing himself/herself from his/her friends. Talking is essential to prevent self-harming and developing a borderline personality disorder.

I think Susan's comment comes quite close to the writer's message, because the article wants people to become aware of the problem which is not easily solved as the adolescents at risk may not ask for help and may end up in a vicious circle. To prevent self-harming and suicide, adults should keep an eye on youngsters at risk to guide them away from any dangerous websites and from solitude. As Dr. Bond put it: education and better policing could tackle the threat (ll. 75–77).

d) The editorial staff had to choose between the photograph on page 51 and another one presenting a set of scales showing the back of a teenager and a dangerously low weight of 43 kg (approx. 94 pounds). Which of the photos seems to match the article more effectively?

To my mind, both photos _would be useful for this article_ because _they show quite clearly that some hard facts about weight and waist measurement are of major importance. On the whole I would perhaps prefer the photo with the scales, as it illustrates more clearly the life-threatening elements of anorexia._

Film CD-ROM, Track 3

6 Disfigured – Learning to Accept Your Body (1)

This video is a scene from a film which seems to be a documentary on **the first meeting** of a group of fat people attending a *Fat Acceptance Group*. The protagonists are the group leader and Lydia, both obese, and Darcy, a young thin woman recovering from anorexia.

Watch this first scene and take notes on the aspects mentioned below. Do not write full sentences. You will see the film clip twice. First look at the task. After the second viewing complete your notes and answer the questions below. There is an example at the beginning.

Example: What kind of people are meeting here and what features do they have in common?

Mostly women – only one man – they are all fat

1. What is the aim of the Fat Acceptance Group according to the group leader?

2. How does Lydia disturb the group feeling of solidarity?

3. Why does the group leader not like this idea?

4. How does the group react to Darcy's entering the room and sitting at the back of the group?

5. How does the group react to Darcy's intention of becoming a member of their group?

6. Why does the group leader want to exclude Darcy at once?

7. What is Darcy's main argument for wanting to belong in this group although she is not fat?

8. How does Lydia try to prevent Darcy's exclusion?

9. When the group leader sends Darcy away, she says twice she is sorry. Do you believe her?

10. What do you think about Lydia's idea of a walking group for fat people?

11. "I like the way our group leader handled this meeting." Do you agree?

Film CD-ROM, Track 3

6 Disfigured – Learning to Accept Your Body (1)

1. What is the aim of the Fat Acceptance Group according to the group leader?

To be accepted by society without having to lose weight

2. How does Lydia disturb the group feeling of solidarity?

She announces her intention of starting up a "non-competitive" walking group for fat people at Venice Beach

3. Why does the group leader not like this idea?

Because she thinks that Lydia wants to lose weight/to slim/to abide by the norm of society, which she does not want to

4. How does the group react to Darcy's entering the room and sitting at the back of the group?

They try to ignore her

5. How does the group react to Darcy's intention of becoming a member of their group?

Mostly aggressively, except Lydia

6. Why does the group leader want to exclude Darcy at once?

Darcy is extremely thin, the leader is jealous/envious of her, Darcy is the detested image and idol of a thin society.

7. What is Darcy's main argument for wanting to belong in this group although she is not fat?

Because all of them feel under pressure from a society that wants people to meet a certain ideal, but instead they should accept that people come in "different shapes and sizes"

8. How does Lydia try to prevent Darcy's exclusion?

By asking whether they should set a weight limit

9. When the group leader sends Darcy away, she says twice she is sorry. Do you believe her?

No, she is lying as she is happy to get rid of her, telling her quite bluntly to get out

10. What do you think about Lydia's idea of a walking group for fat people?

As Lydia does "not feel comfortable doing sports with people who are fat", such a group would be a good starting point for some healthy exercise and good company. If she lost some weight that would be a good side effect. But concerning this issue, the group leader is of a different opinion, because she wants to change the American society's craze/ideal of youth and slimness.

11. "I like the way our group leader handled this meeting." Do you agree?

The answer depends on the student's general opinion on resolute people who often take quick decisions (here: to chuck Darcy out at the very beginning). She addresses Lydia, "I don't want to jump on you!" which betrays her aggressiveness and authoritarian attitude. As a group leader and mediator she should be less emotional and less dominant.

Film CD-ROM, Track 3

6 Disfigured – Learning to Accept Your Body (2)

The last scene of the film shows Lydia founding her own self-help group – her aim is to make the participants accept and love their bodies.

a) Fill in the gaps in the text below with the following words. Some words/phrases can be used several times.

bodies • body parts • overweight • love • underweight • feelings • beauty • strange • acceptable • try • hate • fix them up • beautiful • us • pathetic • miraculous • accept

"We are here to talk about our ______________ (1). ______________ (2) or ______________ (3) or changing weight – or maybe not having anything to do with ______________ (4) at all ... Maybe we should start with making a list of all our ______________ (5) ______________ (6), just to get our ______________ (7) out. But more importantly, I think that we just need to find a way to let our ______________ (8) in – because these bodies, they're ______________ (9). And I don't understand how we can live in them all day, every day and still find them so ______________ (10). How can we ______________ (11) them? They're ______________ (12), and ______________ (13), and ______________ (14), and ______________ (15). And everything that we have in life we get through them.
I don't know, maybe we can help each other ______________ (16) a little. Sooner or later we just have to find a way to ______________ (17) them for what they are. To be able to ______________ (18) what that looks like for each one of us. I don't think that's going to happen any time soon – but we have to ______________ (19), we just have to ______________ (20). And I can't do that myself ..."

Follow-up activity

b) "... everything that we have in life we get through them [our bodies]." State whether you agree or disagree with Lydia's statement.

Film CD-ROM, Track 3

6 Disfigured – Learning to Accept Your Body (2)

a) (1) bodies; (2) overweight; (3) underweight; (4) weight; (5) acceptable; (6) body parts; (7) feelings; (8) feelings; (9) us; (10) strange; (11) hate ; (12) beautiful; (13) pathetic; (14) miraculous; (15) sad; (16) fix them up; (17) love; (18) accept; (19) try; (20) try

Follow-up activity

b) The student's answer depends mainly on her/his inclination towards either the American way/overestimation of physical attraction or the more classical conception (mens sana in corpore sano) or a combination of both.

One example:

Of course, I would partly agree with this statement as in my generation – with reference to the example of the online social networks (facebook, etc.) – personal and physical attraction go hand in hand. But I would not go as far as the group leader by saying that obese people are discriminated against or even hated because of a certain role model. Even in the USA (look at some successful obese singers) people are not only accepted because of their physical/outward appearance. This may be different with models.

I think the world should pay more attention to a person's mind and soul. But business and personal relationships are so short-lived or transient that the time to get to know a person and his/her personality is so short-dated. It is this lack of time that sadly accounts for the superficial and shallow perception or idea of a human being.

Film CD-ROM, Track 4

6 Disfigured – Learning to Accept Your Body (3)

This video is a scene from a film which seems to be a documentary on a group of obese people attending a *Fat Acceptance Group*. You have already watched the first scene about the first meeting, during which Darcy, a new arrival to the group, was made to leave because she was not obese. In this scene (Lessons/Lessons Begin), Lydia, who had tried to support Darcy in her attempt to join the group, comes and sees Darcy at home.

Watch this first scene and take notes on the aspects mentioned below. Do not write full sentences. You will see the film clip twice. First look at the task. After the second viewing complete your notes and answer the questions below. There is an example at the beginning.

a) What is the atmosphere like when they meet in Darcy's living room?

quite relaxed – Lydia compliments Darcy on the 'huge' room and Darcy offers her cookies – which Lydia rejects – while Darcy recommends them – which Lydia jokingly questions insinuating that Darcy has certainly not eaten any of these cookies – they laugh about this and Darcy invites her to sit down.

1. What are Lydia's reasons for coming and seeing Darcy?

2. What kind of help does Lydia ask for?

3. Why does Darcy reject Lydia's request?

4. How does the film show that the protagonists' emotions are boiling up?

5. Why is Lydia so desperate?

6. What does Lydia learn about Darcy's experiences with therapies?

7. How do we get to know that Lydia does not believe her?

8. What do both agree upon concerning therapy?

9. What happens some days later?

10. How does Darcy introduce this gadget to Lydia?

11. What does Lydia think about it?

12. Do you think they will stay friends? Give reasons.

Follow-up activity

b) Imagine one of Lydia's group is your best friend and that she has written an email to you telling you that she has signed up – as her last resort – for an operation on her stomach to reduce her intake of food. How would you try to talk her out of it? Write that email.

Film CD-ROM, Track 4

6 Disfigured – Learning to Accept Your Body (3)

a)

1. What are Lydia's reasons for coming and seeing Darcy?

She wants Darcy to help her.

2. What kind of help does Lydia ask for?

She wants Darcy to give her lessons on anorexia.

3. Why does Darcy reject Lydia's request?

She feels hurt/cannot understand that strange idea of hers, as anorexia is a serious illness that cannot be stopped.

4. How does the film show that the protagonists' emotions are boiling up?

Both are in tears – use foul language ("fucked-up thing, fucked-up world")

5. Why is Lydia so desperate?

She wants to come to terms with her obesity ("I don't want to stay that way for the rest of my days")

6. What does Lydia learn about Darcy's experiences with therapies?

That they did not work/12 years with four different therapists were of no avail/useless/futile.

7. How do we get to know that Lydia does not believe her?

She asks whether those had been real therapists (certified).

8. What do both agree upon concerning therapy?

That therapies cannot help them, they have to help themselves.

9. What happens some days later?

They meet again/they have different clothes on/sit on a couch and unpack a new set of scales.

10. How does Darcy introduce this gadget to Lydia?

"This is your new best friend."

11. What does Lydia think about it?

She does not agree while asking, "And what are you?" suggesting that not the scales but Darcy is her best friend now.

12. Do you think they will stay friends? Give reasons.

Of course, they will stay friends, because they have a common enemy: their eating disorders. Their new set of scales will be an unemotional judge of their progress.

Follow-up activity

b) Imagine one of Lydia's group is your best friend and that she has written an email to you telling you that she has signed up – as her last resort – for an operation on her stomach to reduce her intake of food. How would you try to talk her out of it? Write that email.

Dear Betty,

Don't do it. For one thing, it is obvious that an operation always involves a high risk. Apart from this you should know that it would reduce your food intake only for a short time, if you took up your old habit of nibbling all the time. A friend of a friend of mine did the same as you want to and a year after her operation she was as obese as before.

Believe me, you have to make up your mind to change your eating habits and then quite slowly, of course, you will reduce your weight. We could do this together, if you want to.

Take care.

Much love

XXX

Students' Book, pp. 63 ff.

7 John Green
Looking for Alaska

This excerpt from the novel *Looking for Alaska* is the narrative of a 16-year-old boy about his arrival at his new boarding school far away from home in the USA and his farewell to his parents, who have taken him and his belongings there.

a) Read the passage and tick off ☒ the right answer. Sometimes more than one answer may be correct.

1. The text deals with …

- ☐ a boy called Miles Halter.
- ☐ a student who is about to leave university.
- ☐ a story set in Florida.
- ☐ a narrative taking place in Alabama.

2. The scene being described is about …

- ☐ his parents' separation and divorce.
- ☐ his father's experience at the same school.
- ☐ his mother's overprotective behaviour.
- ☐ his arrival at the boarding school.

b) Which of the statements are correct? Tick off ☒ the right answer. Only one is correct.

1.	**The boy's parents …**	**True**	**False**
	are happy to get rid of him.		
	are in a hurry to leave him.		
	do love their son.		
	take the plane to return home.		
2.	**The boy's room in the school …**		
	is a large, well-furnished room.		
	seems to be more comfortable than he imagined.		
	has got a private bathroom.		
	is cool because of the air-conditioning.		

Follow-up activity

c) As their homework some students handed in the following summaries. Which one do you think is the best one?

Robin
Miles Halter and his parents arrive at his new school in Alabama, where he is to stay on his own for at least a year. They are astonished and even shocked that it is even hotter there than at home in Florida. Miles does not like his new room, because it is tiny and does not have air-conditioning. Both his parents seem to treat him like a child as his mother wants to make his bed and his father gives him unnecessary advice on how to behave properly. Their farewell is clumsy and Miles is looking forward to making new friends.

Camila
A boy called Miles Halter is taken to a boarding school far away from home. Miles is taken aback and even shocked about his uncomfortable tiny room and the terrible heat, which he had not expected. He is looking forward to making new friends and to being separated from his parents who seem to regret leaving him behind.

Charlotte
The text deals with the arrival of 16-year-old Miles Halter at his boarding school, where his parents have taken him. He has mixed feelings about saying good-bye to his parents and about his room which is not up to his expectations. His parents clumsily take leave, but Miles is fantasizing about making new friends.

To my mind, __________'s text ____ because

____

____

____

____

____

____

d) If you had the chance to spend a year at a boarding school far away from home, would you take it? Give reasons.

____

____

____

____

____

____

____

Students' Book, pp. 63 ff.

7 John Green
Looking for Alaska

a)

1. The text deals with ...

- [x] a boy called Miles Halter.
- [ ] a student who is about leaving university.
- [ ] a story set in Florida.
- [x] a narrative taking place in Alabama.

2. The scene being described is about ...

- [ ] his parents' separation and divorce.
- [ ] his father's experience at the same school.
- [x] his mother's overprotective behaviour.
- [x] his arrival at the boarding school.

b)

1.	**The boy's parents ...**	**True**	**False**
	are happy to get rid of him.		X
	are in a hurry to leave him.		X
	do love their son.	X	
	take the plane to return home.		X
2.	**The boy's room in the school ...**		
	a large, well-furnished room.		X
	seems to be more comfortable than he imagined.		X
	has got a private bathroom.	X	
	is cool because of the air-conditioning		X

Follow-up activity

c)

To my mind, Charlotte's text is quite good as she comes up with the main facts and summarizes the descriptive parts, the dialogue and the interior monologue. There is only one important point which is lacking and that is the impact of the heat on the characters' disposition/feelings/state of mind. Camilla's text is not bad, either, as she included this last point and sticks to the facts and keeps things short and uses formal language. Robin did understand the text but tends more to retelling it than to summarizing it.

d)

Well, I would take it, but I have only a fat chance of that as my parents would argue against sending me away for religious reasons. I think a stay at a boarding school would help me to take on more responsibility. I would not say that my family hampers me, but certain restrictions, certain limits, "some guidance" as they call it, have prevented me from making experiences and mistakes. For mistakes are important, too. You cannot develop a sense of self-reliance without having previously made mistakes and tested your limits.

or:

Of course not, because I hate uncertainties and the consequences of losing a year at school, as my friends and class mates would be one year ahead of me and I would not be able to take A-levels with them. This would mean different courses and teachers at home and abroad. No, definitely not a good idea, to my mind. And above all, I would not be able to see and meet my girlfriend for such a long time that I would be afraid of losing her.

Audio CD 1, Track 8

8 Gossip
Get a Job

The song "Get a Job" by Gossip, an American Indie Band (standing for 'Independent Rock Band'), made a breakthrough in 2006 and has become quite famous in Germany and other European countries lately. This has to do with its lead singer Beth Ditto, who is proud to be a lesbian and a real 'heavyweight' with her 100 kg, who – in spite of her outward appearance, uncommon in the world of fashion – became a fashion icon. Reporting on a successful performance in Munich on May 9, 2012, the German national paper "Die Welt" ran the banner: "Beth Ditto is on the right track to become Elton John" and the subtitle read: "From Freak-show to Mainstream".

adorable *bewunderungswürdig* – **cute** *niedlich* – **to push thirty** *(infml.)* to be close to the age of thirty – **gotta** *(infml.)* to have to – **gonna** *(infml.)* going to – **rent** *Miete* – **lack of sth.** *Mangel an* – **inheritance** *Erbschaft, Nachlass*

a) During the first listening, try to concentrate on a general understanding of the text and give your first impression very briefly by making notes on the following topics:

good song because ____________________

average song because ____________________

bad song because ____________________

b) After the second listening, try to put down more details on the following subjects:

the singer represents someone who ____________________

the other girl, who is she? ____________________

c) Listen carefully a third time and find out to whom the quotes refer: either to the singer or to the other girl:

... like to stay and party when • ... ask for the rent • ... just had • ... hair done • ... poor little rich • ... need to work very hard • ... don't know where the money went • ... with ... lack of experience • ... gotta try try try • ... spending other people's money • ... not so cute any more • ... pushing thirty • ... know it's hard but • ... sleeping in

Put the quotes into the grid below and say what kind of characteristics they highlight. One example is given:

quote	singer (s) girl (g)	characteristic quality
poor little rich [girl]	g	in spite of being rich having bad characteristics

quote	singer (s) girl (g)	characteristic quality

Follow-up activity

d) Write a short characterization of the "rich girl" and prove – if you are able to – your findings by quotes from the text.

e) To what degree do you think the characters to be realistic or believable?

f) Imagine the 'rich girl' leaves the singer and wants to take revenge by reproaching and blaming him/her in her fare-well note. Write this short letter.
Bye, my love, I'm leaving you because ______

g) Some students handed in their comments on the song and/or the video. Read the texts and say which one would get the better mark. Give reasons.

Chris

In the song, Ditto calls upon a girl living on her rich parents' money to get a job to support herself. I don't like the song – I mean the text. The music is o.k., but the lyrics are rather unrealistic, even if Beth, as a lesbian, might think that such criticism might be a good idea for the young people in the audience. Sure, she and her band had started at the bottom and know about making ends meet on minimum wages. The video is really blunt showing her in all kinds of jobs after having gone through the offers in the paper with inflated promises. There was an offer 'Train for a dentist' which was the only serious occupation depicted and that, too, was ridiculed or treated with irony as Beth – grimacing wildly – was shown attacking a patient on a dentist's chair more in the way of Dracula looking for blood or revenge. The final touch was a shot of loads of money pouring down on Beth or someone else. Well, typically American: Money makes the world go round. And that's it. Message – zero!

Betty

When I read the text first, I had the impression the song was meant to present some man reproaching his girl-friend for her rather negative characteristics. Moreover, I had a feeling that the constant repetition of 'Get a job' might be an ironical version of some parents' slogan about chucking their child out of the house. Watching the video was then a bit of a shock as the singer turned out to be a female of oversize proportions making fun of the imperative 'Get a job', as she was singing and dancing in a lascivious way, showing a lot of flesh while being decipted working in several jobs from low-paid servant at a fast food restaurant to the fishy occupation in a brothel or offering telephone sex.

To my mind, __________'s text ____

____

____

____

____

____

h) Against the background of the text, finish the following if-clauses using the right tenses in the main clauses.

1. If my parents had not spoilt me, ______________________________

2. If I find a good job, ______________________________

3. If you loved me, ______________________________

4. If you had not shown such a lack of experience, ______________________________

5. If you were not so hard on me, ______________________________

6. If the unemployment rate were not so high, ______________________________

7. If this song is a success, ______________________________

8. If you forgave me my sluttishness (*Schlampigkeit*), ______________________________

i) The rich girl and the singer have a row

Either use the adjectives or form adverbs and add them to the sentences below.

polite • ironic • nervous • excited • cheerful • kind • angry • miserable • bitter • happy • furious • arrogant

"Ha! **You** go to work!" the rich girl laughed.
Example: … *the rich girl laughed arrogantly.*

1. "Well, you know someone has to pay the rent!" the singer answered.

____

____

2. "Would you hand me that hairbrush, please," she said to her friend.

____

____

3. "I want to go out. My life here tastes! ______________________________!"

____

4. He said, "I thought you did not have any money left."

____

5. "That's right. I don't have any money left for the rent," she snapped.

____

____

6. "That's what I thought all the time," he said. "You go partying and I'm the fool who brings home the money."

____

____

7. She said, "You know you are so mean always reproaching me for spending some money."

____

____

8. "I really have had enough of you. Just get a job or leave my flat!" he retorted (*scharf erwidern*).

____

____

Audio CD 1, Track 8

8 Gossip
Get a Job

a) During the first listening, try to concentrate on a general understanding of the text and give your first impression very briefly by making notes on the following topics:

good song because: music good, etc.

average song because: e.g. music does not fit the lyrics

bad song because: story not believable, etc.

b) After the second listening, try to put down more details on the following subjects:

the singer represents someone who has a girl-friend living on her parents' money/reprimands that girl/thinks that a job would teach her responsibility

the other girl, who is she? The rich girl is living on her parents' money/not able to support herself, does not earn any money, is only interested in wasting time/leisure activities

c) Put the quotes into the grid below and say what kind of characteristics they highlight.

quote	singer(s) girl (g)	characteristic quality
[I'd] like to stay and party but I gotta work	s	dutiful, reliable
… just had [your] hair done	g	is just a dummy, only interested in make-up
oh girl you need to work real hard	g	childish, naïve, childlike
… when [I] ask for the rent	s	wants to guide her on the right track
… with your lack of experience	g	has not yet worked, no one will employ her
[you] don't know where the money went	g	careless with money, irresponsible
[you] gotta try try try	g	finding a job will be difficult
… spending other people's money	g	careless with money, irresponsible
… not so cute	g	her attractiveness has gone
… [you're] sleeping in	g	while the singer is at work, she is lazy
[now that you're] pushing thirty	g	now it is time to learn how to earn money
[I] know it's hard but …	s	thinks that the change will be difficult for her

Follow-up activity

d) Write a short characterization of the "rich girl" and prove – if you are able to – your findings by quotes from the text.

From the very beginning, the singer does not seem to like the "rich girl" as she is a bit stupid (ll. 1 f.) but at the same time she is cunning and sly, living at other people's expense. She was a beauty when she was young, but now in her late twenties, her good looks (not cute any more) are fading. It is about time for her to start working to support herself. But finding a job will prove to be difficult as she has never worked before. So far, her only concern had been her looks and her parties. She has lost track of her money. She is the typical happy-go-lucky girl, a real sponger.

e) To what degree do you think the characters to be realistic or believable?

Both characters don't seem to be realistic or believable. Such an overdose of bourgeois/middle-class morals is just too much to bear for many, especially when it comes from the mouth of a declared lesbian.
Nevertheless, I keep wondering at the tremendous success of the song and the video so far, in which the slogan "Get a job" is repeated again and again and cannot be ignored. Maybe others do see the song differently and that may be the reason for the band's success. Perhaps the song is actually being critical of middle-class norms. Or is it simply a straight forward criticism of the behaviour of young women who live at the experse of others? There are various ways of interpreting this song and your view will determine how realistic you find the presentation.

f) Imagine the 'rich girl' leaves the singer and wants to take revenge by reproaching and blaming him/her in her fare-well note. Write this short letter.

Bye, my love, I'm leaving you because you were quite blunt in telling me you had enough of me. O.K. before you chuck me out, I'm going on my own. But you could have told me earlier that you wanted me to take a job and live a typical middle-class life. Sorry, that is not my cup of tea.
This is not my style as I am not made to be a homebody. All I want is someone to love and support me and I am offering – in exchange – to be a loving and devoted woman.
You were quite mean to reproach me for my inheritance. In reality, it is my parents who are responsible for having spoilt me.
So, goodbye,
Much love
Trish XXX

g) Some students handed in their comments on the song and/or the video. Read the texts and say which one would get the better mark. Give reasons.

To my mind, Chris's text is better as it starts off with a good summary and provides a very personal comment and evaluation displaying a lot of understanding.
However, I also like Betty's comment, although it is perhaps too personal on the whole. Her arguments are well-founded.

h) Against the background of the text, finish the following if-clauses using the right tenses in the main clauses.

1. If my parents had not spoilt me, changing my life would have been much easier for me.

2. If I find a good job, I will pay you back all the money you lent me.

3. If you loved me, you would not be so reproachful.

4. If you had not shown such a lack of experience, you would have been employed easily.

5. If you were not so hard on me, I could go on loving you/staying with you.

6. If the unemployment rate were not so high, I would get a job in no time.

7. If this song is a success, we will stay friends and make some money this way.

8. If you forgave me my sluttishness, we would not have to end our relationship.

i) **The rich girl and the singer have a row**
Either use the adjectives or form adverbs and add them to the sentences below:

1. "Well, you know someone has to pay the rent!" the singer answered.

"Well, you know someone has to pay the rent!" the singer answered angrily/bitterly/arrogantly/miserably.

2. "Would you hand me that hairbrush, please," she said to her friend.

"Would you hand me that hairbrush, please," she politely/kindly said to her friend.

3. "I want to go out. My life here tastes bitter!

4. He said, "I thought you did not have any money left."

He said ironically/angrily/furiously/bitterly, "I thought you did not have any money left.

5. "That's right. I don't have any money left for the rent,", she snapped.

"That's right. I don't have any money left for the rent," she snapped nervously.

6. "That's what I thought all the time," he said. "You go partying and I'm the fool who brings home the money."

"That's what I thought all the time," he said ironically/angrily …

7. She said, "You know you are so mean, always reproaching me for spending some money."

She said angrily/nervously/furiously/bitterly, "You know you are so mean always reproaching me for spending some money."

8. "I really have had enough of you. Just get a job or leave my flat!" he retorted.

I really have had enough of you. Just get a job or leave my flat!" he retorted arrogantly/furiously/angrily.

Students' Book, pp. 80 ff.

9 EU Migration to Germany – *Sprechen Sie Job*?

abridgements *Kürzungen* – **influx** *Zulauf* – **to swap** *tauschen* – **mock warrant of apprehension** *Steckbrieffälschung* – **moustache** *Schnurrbart*; **OECD** Organisation for Economic Co-operation and Development, an international economic organisation of 34 states with its headquarters in Paris

This newspaper article taken from the Economist – with minor abridgements – deals with the influx of skilled workers into Europe and the difficulties of one European swapping countries in search of a job.

a) Study the article at hand and the image below and fill in a mock warrant of apprehension in the form of a 'wanted poster'. Justify your entry by referring to information provided in the article.

	references
name of the wanted person Daniel Gómez Garcia	l. 3
nationality	
gender	
outward appearance	
age	
reason for his being on the run	
possible whereabouts	
education	
knowledge of languages	
other personal abilities or qualities	
work experience	
last country of residence	

Follow-up activity

b)

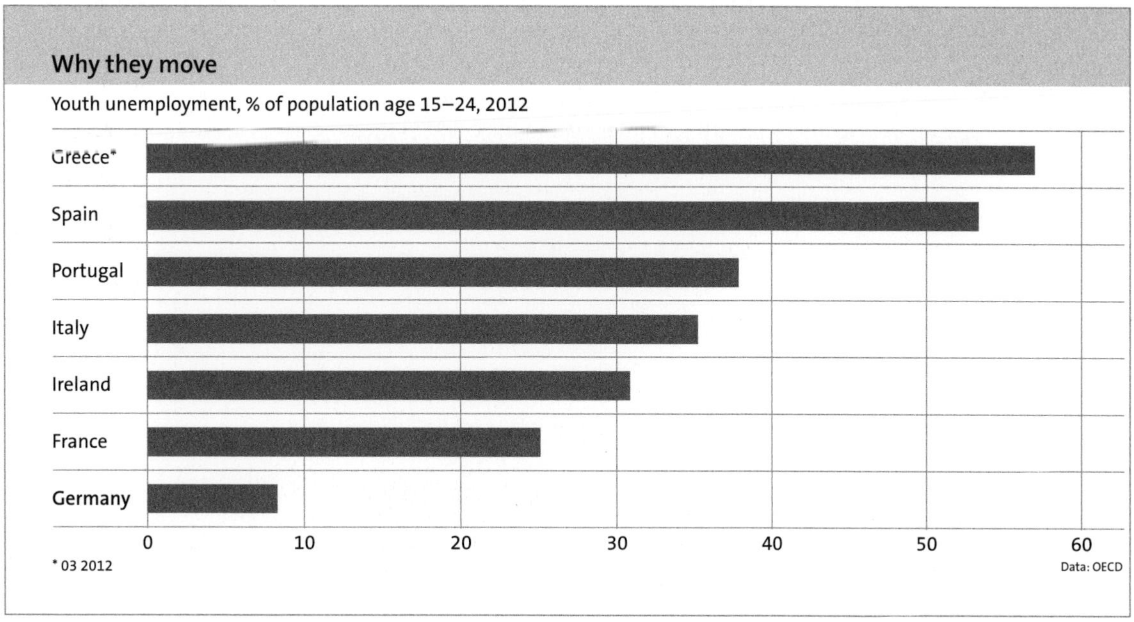

1. Identify the type of chart or graph you see above. Give the source.

2. Describe the chart/graph: What is it about? What does it refer to? What information does it give?

3. Draw conclusions from the chart/graph.

Students' Book, pp. 80 ff.

9 EU Migration to Germany – *Sprechen Sie Job*?

a) Study the article at hand and the image below and fill in a *mock warrant of apprehension* a 'wanted poster': Justify your entry by referring to information provided in the article.

	references
name of the wanted person Daniel Gómez Garcia	l. 3
nationality Spanish	l. 6 f.
gender male	ll. 3, 9
outward appearance black hair, Southerner, moustache	poster
age 23	l. 3
reason for his being on the run high unemployment in Spain, looking for a job	ll. 10, 18, 55
possible whereabouts somewhere in Europe	ll. 13 f.
education school in Spain and studies in the USA	ll. 7, 8
knowledge of languages fluent Spanish, passable English, a little German	ll. 7, 8
other personal abilities or qualities IT, knowledge of Excel, accounting experience, flexibility	ll. 15, 16 whole article
work experience internship at the Spanish embassy employment at a holiday-rental firm and as an accountant	ll. 12 f., 14
last country of residence Germany	ll. 33–55

Follow-up activity

b)

1. It is a bar chart and its source is the OECD and it offers its findings from 2012.

2. The chart shows the percentages of youth unemployment in some European countries in order to demonstrate why many young people are forced to leave their native countries to get a job elsewhere.
   The article can be directly set against the background of the chart. It demonstrates effectively that the Greek youth unemployment rate is about 7 times higher than in Germany, while Spanish youth unemployment (more than 50 %) is worse than that of France, which has "only" 25 %. Germany has the lowest figures.

3. The conclusion is quite simple: the country where business is thriving (Germany) has the best employment rate for young people, while – as for instance in Greece – suffering businesses and poor or no GNP (gross national product) growth lead to increasing and high unemployment. The consequence is the influx (migration) of unemployed Europeans into Germany.

Film CD-ROM, Tracks 5, 6

10 Lucy Alibar, Benh Zeitlin
Beasts of the Southern Wild

The film and the screenplay script remind the audience and readers of the Apocalypse (Bible) or the images of the disaster of Hurricane Katrina in the gulf of Louisiana. The setting is a bleak corner of the bayou*, called the Bathtub*, where a six-year-old girl, Hushpuppy, and her father Wink, a hard-drinking fisherman, make a living and where Hushpuppy goes to a make-shift school. There the schoolmistress, Miss Bathsheba, teaches the local children mostly about the imminent radical changes to the environment, caused by global warming and setting free most animals from the ice age.

*__bayou__ marshy, boggish land, *sumpfiger Flussarm* – *__Bathtub__ nickname for an isolated area in the bayou – *__Aurochs__ *Ur-Rind*

a) Before watching the scene from the film, study the text and the vocabulary and make some notes after the first reading:

First impression of the structure of the screenplay: strange because ______________________

____

____

What happens? ______________________

____

____

Why do Hushpuppy's friends flee? ______________________

____

____

How does Hushpuppy cope with the Aurochs? ______________________

____

____

What do the Aurochs do? ______________________

____

____

____

What happens to Hushpuppy's father? ______________________

____

____

b) View the extract from the film and make notes …

Which part of the scene impressed you most? ______

What do you think about the music/sound track? ______

What is the dominant atmosphere like? ______

c) Several times Hushpuppy is shown close-up and her gaze seems to be … when she is facing the Aurochs. Choose adequate adjectives from the list below and say what thoughts and feelings may have been on Hushpuppy's mind.

warm • dissatisfied • desolate • bright • focused • happy • dark • sad • melancholic • nostalgic • cool thoughtful • confident • aggressive • contented • satisfied • scared • unafraid • soothing

d) Watch the scene again, rework your notes. What differences between the text and film version did you recognize?

Follow-up activity

e) Find a different ending to this film scene.

f) What struck you most when watching track 6 (Making of ...)?

g) Leaving the cinema, one spectator said – after watching the film – that it had forsaken its potential to warn effectively about global warming because the Aurochs were unrealistic and destroyed everything. What do you think?

h) Grammar and style: Hypotaxis
A good way to improve your style is matching two short sentences by using participles. Try to do that with the following sentences, but be careful: the participle does not always work. An example is given at the beginning.

Hushpuppy and her friends were strolling through high grass. They watched out for the Aurochs.
While strolling through high grass, they watched out for the Aurochs.

1. Hushpuppy turns. She catches a glimpse of something massive moving behind the distant oaks.

2. The kids turn and hustle down the ridge. The distant trampling is growing louder.

3. The Aurochs bear down on Hushpuppy from behind. They grow inconceivably large.

4. Hushpuppy does not flinch. The Aurochs stares face to face with Hushpuppy.

5. Wink looks at Hushpuppy in reverence. He knows it's the last time.

6. Hushpuppy squeezes Wink. She does not let go.

7. He embraces her. Wink's hand trembles on her back.

Film CD-ROM, Tracks 5, 6

10 Lucy Alibar
Beasts of the Southern Wild

a) Before watching the scene from the film, study the text and the vocabulary and make some notes after the first reading:

First impression:

strange/difficult because I've never read a screenplay script with such long stage directions and so little dialogue

What happens?

The girl seems determined/resolute to face the danger/does not cry for help

Why do Hushpuppy's friends flee?

They seem to know (because of their teacher) that danger/their death is imminent/are first confident that they will get away/when Aurochs are near they start crying/run away

How does Hushpuppy cope with the Aurochs?

H. is at first scared/does not run away/is determined to face them

What do the Aurochs do?

They stop short of attacking H./when she turns round the leading Aurochs is impressed/is stared down by H./ kneels down in front of H.

What happens to Hushpuppy's father?

Wink is taken aback by H.'s fearlessness/is about to die

b) View the extract from the film and make notes ...

Which part of the scene impressed you most?

Hushpuppy facing up to the leading Aurochs.

What do you think about the music/sound track?

I like the music/it never promotes aggression/not even when the attack of the Aurochs is imminent/music may reflect Hushpuppy's thoughts and emotions/stampede of the Aurochs/the end of the music could well symbolize the end of Hushpuppy's fear/the composition of the music serves well to maintain full attention on the sounds made by the Aurochs and on Hushpuppy's words

What is the dominant atmosphere like?

There is no dominant atmosphere, because it changes quite often/first peaceful (the girls walking)/asking for attention – crescendo – scary/sad and deathly (Wink's deathbed)/dangerous (advancing Aurochs – fleeing/crying girls)/angry (Hushpuppy looking in the direction of her father) climax (Hushpuppy facing the Aurochs)/unclear, mixed atmosphere because of stalemate (Hushpuppy staring down the Aurochs)/soothing and peaceful (Aurochs kneeling down), relaxed (Hushpuppy's reconciliatory words) peaceful & determined (Hushpuppy ready to face Wink)

c) Several times Hushpuppy is shown close-up and her gaze seems to be ... when she is facing the Aurochs. Choose those adequate adjectives from the list below and say what thoughts and feelings may have been on Hushpuppy's mind.

Shortly before turning round, Hushpuppy is focused and unafraid as she seems determined to overcome her fear and face the Aurochs and to find out whether Miss Bathsheba's reports were true. She is eye to eye with the leading Aurochs and succeeds in staring it down, in dominating the leading Aurochs, which then submits itself to Hushpuppy by kneeling down. Her face seems to express soothing sadness as the animals turn away (I gotta take care of mine.).

d) Watch the scene again, rework your notes. What differences between the text and film version did you recognize?

First of all, there is a different ending. While the scene in the film breaks off quite suddenly, the text has 30 lines (one column) more with Wink dying and a final comment by Hushpuppy. Secondly, while the film version does not give any hint why the Aurochs give in to the girl whereas the text gives an interpretation of their actions, thoughts and intentions: The Aurochs lowers her head with respect. Her eyes well with emotion, recognizing one of her own. A ferocious warrior. (ll. 44–46)

Follow-up activity

e) Find a different ending to this film scene.

Several endings are possible, either positive or negative ones, normal or deus ex machina resolutions, for example: Wink's wife coming back by helicopter to take him to hospital and save them all from drowning.
Or: A tornado kills them all.
Or: Wink getting better and clinging to life because of his responsibility for Hushpuppy.

f) What struck you most when watching track 6 (Making of ...)?

Personal views cannot be predicted easily. One example: I was amazed at the technical tricks, but most of all by the cleverness of the pigs which could be trained like dogs and were even more adaptable than dogs when swimming with those masks on.

g) Leaving the cinema, one spectator said – after watching the film – that it had forsaken its potential to warn effectively about global warming because the Aurochs were unrealistic and destroyed everything. What do you think?

This spectator obviously wanted to have a documentary on global warming. The film, however, had different aims as it did not want to offer realism, but – as a piece of art – to combine magical or fantastic elements (here the Aurochs) with realistic setting. Experts call this 'Magic Realism'. The film is – above all – about a small girl who has to overcome great fear, when confronted by dangerous situations and when losing her father.

h) Grammar and style: Hypotaxis

1. Hushpuppy turns. She catches a glimpse of something massive moving behind the distant oaks.

When turning, she catches a glimpse ...

2. The kids turn and hustle down the ridge. The distant trampling is growing louder.

(impossible)

3. The Aurochs bear down on Hushpuppy from behind. They grow inconceivably large.

Bearing down on H., the Aurochs grow inconceivably large.

4. Hushpuppy does not flinch. The Aurochs stares face to face with Hushpuppy.

(impossible)

5. Wink looks at Hushpuppy in reverence. He knows it's the last time.

Looking at H. in reverence, Wink knows it's the last time.

6. Hushpuppy squeezes Wink. She does not let go.

Squeezing Wink, she does not let go.

7. He embraces her. Wink's hand trembles on her back.

While embracing her, Wink's hand trembles on her back.

Audio CD 1, Track 12

11 John Irving
Trying to Save Piggy Sneed

This extract is part of a collection of short stories in which the author explains how he became a writer. At the centre of the story is Piggy Sneed, who – because of his retardation – has lost his ability to speak and is a garbage collector, has a pig farm and is teased and chased by the children of Front Street. The author and narrator is one of them.

a) Study the text and collect important characteristic aspects about the people who appear in it. There is an example at the beginning.

character	quote	reference
Piggy Sneed	*retarded garbage collector*	l. 3
First-person-narrator		
Grandmother		
Front Street children		

Follow-up activity

b) By means of the text and the above quotes, write a short characterization of the Front Street children.

c) Listen to the extract and answer the following questions in note form:

1. How did the first-person narrator's attitude towards Piggy Sneed change over the years?

2. What is the symbolic meaning of:

Grandmother:

Sneed:

Front Street children:

Fire-brigade:

The fire (Piggy's barn):

Garbage collector: ____

____

____

3. The text says in ll. 153 f., "I understood that comedy was just another form of condolence." Would that be true for this story?

____

____

____

____

____

____

____

d) The odd one out. Look at the words and find out which one does not belong in this category:

1. garbage dirt muck earth
2. awful dreadful terrible awesome
3. to spray to sprinkle to inject to splash
4. to kill to slaughter to butcher to cull
5. spectacle play happening spree
6. fire place oven stovepipe chimney
7. except for instance such as for example
8. but still likewise however

e) Match the following rhetorical devices with the quotes from the text:

hyperbole • chiasm • alliteration • repetition • metaphor • anaphora • simile • parallelism • climax

1. He raised pigs, he slaughtered pigs; more importantly, he lived with his pigs. ______________________

____

2. We sprayed the trees across the road; we sprayed the woods beyond the pig barn. ______________________
3. It was a windless, bitter cold night, the snow as dry and fine as talcum powder. ______________________
4. He set fire to his own place just to give us a hard time. Think of the hard time we gave him.______________
5. It was the biggest fire that we Front Street children, and even the veterans among the Stratham Volunteers, had ever seen. ______________________

6. He was short, heavy, and strong – he heaved the garbage cans to his back, he hurled their contents onto the wooden, slat-sided truck bed. ______________________________

7. ... that burglar alarm in the heart, which is the late-night ringing telephone – the call to danger __________

8. He was tolerated as a harmless animal is tolerated – by children, he was even indulged, he was even encouraged to be a pig. ______________________________

f) The text below the box is the very beginning of the short story at hand, in which some of the words have been deleted and are now to be found in the box below. Complete the text by filling in the gaps with the words in the box.

memoirs • opportunity • rewriting • spontaneous • language • remember • observation detail • happened • truths • imagination • writer • revision

This is a memoir, but please understand that (to any writer with a good ______________) all ______________ are false. A fiction writer's memory is an especially imperfect provider of detail; we can always imagine a better detail than the one we can ______________. The correct detail is rarely, exactly, what ______________; the most truthful ______________ is what could have happened, or what should have. Half my life is an act of ______________; more than half the act is performed with small changes.

Being a ______________ is a strenuous marriage between careful ______________ and just as carefully imagining the ______________ you haven't had the ______________ to see. The rest is the necessary, strict toiling (*sich quälen*) with the ______________; for me this means writing and ______________ the sentences until they sound as ______________ as good conversation.

Audio CD 1, Track 12

11 John Irving
Trying to Save Piggy Sneed

a) Study the text and collect important characteristic aspects about the people turning up in this text. There is an example at the beginning.

character	quote	reference
Piggy Sneed	retarded garbage collector	l. 3
	he smelled worse than any other man	ll. 5 f.
	you would have to be dead to look worse than Piggy Sneed	l. 8
	he lived on a pig farm. He raised pigs, he slaughtered pigs, he lived *with* his pigs	ll. 12 f.
	he had absorbed [...] certain piglike expressions and gestures	ll. 20–22
	he was short, heavy, and strong	l. 29
	the *piggiest* thing about him was that he could not talk	l. 35
	He grunted. He squealed. He oinked – that was his language.	ll. 38 f.
	like a pig, panicked, lurching at random ... Piggy Sneed would squeal back at us	ll. 47–50
	Piggy Sneed was tolerated ... as a harmless animal is tolerated	ll. 64–66
	was a drunk-driving Piggy Sneed, heading home	ll. 94 f.
First-person-narrator	I can't imitate his sound; it was awful, it made us all ... scream and run and hide.	ll. 54 f.
	I grew older and realized (with regret) the cruelty of children	ll. 58 f.
	I joined some civic organization dedicated to caring for people like Piggy Sneed	ll. 59–61
	I felt so superior to Stratham that it surprises me, now, that I joined the ... Fire Department	ll. 75–77
	I insisted to Grandmother that her kindness to Piggy Sneed had not been overlooked by me	ll. 218–220
	One reason I'm a writer is that I sympathized with our need to do this; I have never been interested in what nonwriters call good and bad 'taste'.	ll. 148–151
	That was when I understood that comedy was just another form of condolence. And then I started it; I began my first story.	ll. 153–155
	I realize that a writer's business is setting fire to Piggy Sneed – and trying to save him again and again; forever.	ll. 230–232
Grandmother	my grandmother's good manners	ll. 1 f.
	to whom my grandmother was always polite and kind	ll. 3 f.
	before my grandmother was moved to the old people's home	l. 209
	My grandmother cut me off.	l. 224
	... if you'd only treated Mr. Sneed with a little human decency when he was alive	ll. 227–229
Front Street children	We children ... would sneak up on him ... We'd surprise him: ... We'd leap out at him ... we'd squeal at him	ll. 41–46
	by children, he was indulged, he was even encouraged to be a pig	ll. 66 f.
	growing older, we Front Street children knew that he was retarded ... we learned that he drank a bit	ll. 68–70
	It [belonging to the Fire Department] made us Front Street children important ... it gave us a status ...	ll. 84–86
	as we overtook him – we the front Street children – I distinctly hear us calling, 'Piggy! Piggy! ...'	ll. 102 f.
	we Front Street children were imagining a larkish, if somewhat retarded spectacle	ll. 106–108

Follow-up activity

b) By means of the text and the above quotes, write a short characterization of the Front Street children.

They are a typical group/band of kids looking for some distraction in a rather dull village without any attraction. Sneed is an easy target for their attacks, their derision/mockery, as he is an outcast in every way: his retardation, his inability to speak, his smell, his 'disgusting' job, his lack of human lodgings. They grew older and learnt that he was retarded, but they did not show any mercy on him and kept on calling him 'Piggy', making him a monster, a kind of Frankenstein. They were even looking forward to him and his round of collecting garbage twice a week ('What a luxury!'). As teenagers they joined – which is common usage in villages – the fire brigade which made them feel important and they enjoyed being important to the full.

c) Listen to the extract and answer the following questions in note form:

1. How did the first-person narrator's attitude towards Piggy Sneed change over the years?

as a child/teenager: unashamed, cruel within the group and in the pursuit of their victim

as an adult: ashamed of his former behaviour, ready to make amends, reason for his literary work

2. What is the symbolic meaning of:

Grandmother: the alter ego of the first-person narrator, deep inside, he knows what is wrong but he has to be told – at a certain age – what has to be done, and what he has done wrong.

Sneed: his name could be split into Piggy's Need and he is in need of support, affection, human warmth, human company, social support etc.

Front Street children: typical group of village kids fooling around, looking for some victim/prey, being quite cruel while mobbing some poor guy like Sneed, but enjoying it ('...He came twice a week. What a luxury!', l. 57).

Fire brigade: the narrator joins another group as a teenager, again in search of some company, some thrill, just another 'Front Street children's' group, but perhaps doing some relief work in order to compensate for their former lapses

The fire: tabula rasa, extinction of an abnormal – animal-like – being, elimination of bad feelings/guilty conscience/former mistakes

Garbage collector: a 'disgusting job' in most peoples's eyes, but a very necessary one, here even twice a week, carried out by an outcast of society

3. The text says in ll. 153 f., "I understood that comedy was just another form of condolence." Would that be true for this story?

The situation when the first-person narrator comes to this conclusion, dawning on him like an epiphany, emerges after the fire has destroyed the barn, its owner and the animals. His mates from Front Street (now in the fire brigade) could not do anything to rescue anybody from the fire and start calling softly for 'Piggy'. And then they cry 'Piggy! Piggy! Piggy! OINK! WEEEE!' This is when the narrator realizes that comedy is just another form of condolence. Despite the seeming comic cruelness of this reaction, he and his friends feel sorry for Piggy deep down in their hearts and in their helplessness express their feeling in this way.

Thus, it becomes clear that what they enjoyed calling in former times – maybe jokingly – just for fun, has become the outcry of loss because of death.

This does not, however, alter the fact that what was fun to them, was a terrible burden to their victim, Sneed, possibly triggering his decision to commit suicide.

d) The odd one out. Look at the words and find out which one does not belong in this category:

1. garbage dirt muck ~~earth~~
2. awful dreadful terrible ~~awesome~~
3. to spray to sprinkle ~~to inject~~ to splash
4. ~~to kill~~ to slaughter to butcher to cull
5. spectacle play happening ~~spree~~
6. fireplace oven ~~stovepipe~~ chimney
7. ~~except~~ for instance such as for example
8. but still ~~likewise~~ however

e) Match the following rhetorical devices with the quotes from the text:

1. He raised pigs, he slaughtered pigs; more importantly, he lived with his pigs.
   anaphora, parallelism, climax
2. We sprayed the trees across the road; we sprayed the woods beyond the pig barn. anaphora
3. It was a windless, bitter cold night, the snow as dry and fine as talcum powder. simile
4. **He** set fire to his own place just to **give us** a hard time. Think of the hard time **we gave him**. chiasm
5. It was the biggest fire that we Front Street children, and even the veterans among the Stratham Volunteers, had ever seen. hyperbole
6. **He** was short, heavy, and strong – **he** heaved the garbage cans to his back, **he** hurled their contents onto the wooden, slat-sided truck bed. alliteration, repetition

7. ... that burglar alarm in the heart, which is the late-night ringing telephone – the call to danger,

metaphor

8. He was **tolerated** as a harmless animal is tolerated – by children, he was **even indulged**, he was **even encouraged** to be a pig. climax

f) The text below the box is the very beginning of the short story at hand, in which some of the words have been deleted and are now to be found in the box below. Complete the text by filling in the gaps with the words in the box.

This is a memoir, but please understand that (to any writer with a good imagination) all memoirs are false. A fiction writer's memory is an especially imperfect provider of detail; we can always imagine a better detail than the one we can remember. The correct detail is rarely, exactly, what happened; the most truthful detail is what could have happened, or what should have. Half my life is an act of revision; more than half the act is performed with small changes.

Being a writer is a strenuous marriage between careful observation and just as carefully imagining the truths you haven't had the opportunity to see. The rest is the necessary, strict toiling with the language; for me this means writing and rewriting the sentences until they sound as spontaneous as good conversation.

Students' Book, pp. 114 ff.

12 Generation Jobless

a) Read the article from the *Economist* and then the summary of the text below, in which some of the words have been deleted. Insert the missing words from the box, which contains three too many. You have 40 minutes for the task.

to estimate *schätzen* – **skilled entry-level workers** (A.E.) *ganz normale gelernte Arbeiter* – **directive** rule – **mentoring** *Betreuung* – **low key** *zurückhaltend, unwillig*

joblessness • apprenticeships • secondary-school education • European countries • vocational education • emerging world • nothing • relationship • unemployed • GDP • mismatch • prejudice • civil-service

The OECD estimates that 26 million young people in the rich countries are **n**ot in **e**mployment, **e**ducation or **t**raining, whom they now call NEETS, while the number of young "inactive" people in the developing countries is ten times higher. If you sum this up, it is a quarter of the world's youth that is doing little or ___________ . Other young people in rich countries only have temporary jobs and have to be supported by benefits, which is very costly to the state and often reduces the ___________ by more than 1%.

Difficulties with their labour markets, low growth and a ___________ between education and work lead to unemployment in the ______________________ (North Africa and Middle Eastern countries). In Europe, Greece, Spain, Italy and France have high youth ______________________. Many countries have difficulties in finding skilled entry-level workers and this is a consequence of poor basic education. Even in richer countries, ___________________________________ is rare among jobless young people.

While France and North Africa do not prepare for jobs in their schools and universities, Germany is aware of the close ___________________ required between education and work, as reflected in its long history of vocational schools and ________________________.

With about 1m NEETs, Britain has almost three times more young unemployed than Germany, which may have to do with the country's ___________ against practical education. Mentoring and training are low key, although work experience is of major importance. Some big firms have made up their minds to train their own new employees. One firm has the dual system, which is part-time job and part-time college. Some use "virtual" experience to train their staff to avoid the cost of ________________________ .

b) Finish the following sentences with the contents of the article in mind:

1. If British pupils had been trained properly, they ____
2. If Greek businesses were successful, young Greeks ____
3. If France prepares French university students for real life, ______________________________________

Students' Book, pp. 114 ff.

12 Generation Jobless

a)

The OECD estimates that 26 million young ones in the rich countries are **n**ot in **e**mployment, **e**ducation or **t**raining, whom they call now NEETS, while the number of young "inactive" people in the developing countries is ten times higher. If you sum this up, it is a quarter of the world's youth that is doing little or nothing. Other young people in rich countries only have temporary jobs and have to be supported by benefits, which is very costly to the state and often reduces the GDP by more than 1%.
Difficulties with their market, low growth and a mismatch between education and work lead to unemployment in the emerging world (North Africa and Middle Eastern countries). In Europe, Greece, Spain, Italy and France have high youth joblessness. Many countries have difficulties in finding skilled entry-level workers and this is a consequence of poor basic education. Even in richer countries, secondary school education is rare among jobless young people.
While France and North Africa do not prepare for jobs in their schools and universities, Germany is aware of the close relationship required between education and work, as reflected in its long history of vocational schools and apprenticeships.
With about 1m NEETs, Britain has almost three times more young unemployed than Germany, which may have to do with the country's prejudice against practical education. Mentoring and training are low key, although work experience is of major importance. Some big firms have made up their minds to train their own new employees. One firm has the dual system, which is part-time job and part-time college. Some use "virtual" experience to train their staff to avoid the cost of vocational education.

b) Finish the following sentences with the contents of the article in mind:

1. If British pupils had been trained properly, they would have got more/better/jobs.

2. If Greek businesses were successful, young Greeks would get jobs/would be employed.

3. If France prepares French university students for real life, they will find more skilled jobs.

Audio CD 2, Track 1

13 Hillary Clinton
Remarks on Youth

Hillary Rodham Clinton, the then U.S Secretary of State, met a lot of young people in a town hall in Tunis, where she delivered the speech on February 25, 2012. This is an extract.
Background knowledge: Almost a year before, Tunisia had revolted against its dictator, Zine el-Abidine Ben Ali, which ignited uprisings in most Northern African countries. Tunisians called for democracy and freedom and the movement went into the history books under the name of "Arab Spring". As the young Tunisians, about 40 % of the Tunisian population – compared to a quarter in Germany – is younger than 25, had an important share in the success of the country's renewal, Clinton appeals especially to the young people of Tunisia to make sure their leaders stay on the path of democracy and meet the promises of reform announced in the Arab Spring.

to determine *bestimmen, festlegen* – **to deny sth. to sb.** *jdm etw. vorenthalten* – **oppressive** *unterdrückerisch* – **aspiration** *Bestreben* – **dynamics** *Dynamik* – **demographics** data relating to the population and the different groups within it – to combat to fight against sth./sb. – **sustainable** *nachhaltig, dauerhaft* – **agenda** *Termin* – **empowerment** support, strengthening, the action of giving responsibility to s.o. – **to marginalise sb.** to make sb. feel as if they were not important – **peril** danger – **youth bulge** a huge amount of young people in a society – **late** here: near the end of a person's life – **to scrape** to manage to get sth. with difficulty – **insufficient** *(fml.)* not important enough, inadequate – **patronage** the system by which an important person gives help or a job to sb. in return for their support *Protektion, Gönnerschaft* – **to reinforce** *etw. verstärken* – **outmoded** old-fashioned, outdated – **reinvigorate** *(fml.) etw. neu beleben* – **grassroots** ordinary people in society or an organization – **tie** a strong connection between people or organisations – **dividend** *Dividende, Gewinnanteil* – **framework** *Rahmenbedingungen* – **advisor** *Berater* – **momentum** the ability to keep increasing and developing; *Eigendynamik* – **Peace Corps** is a volunteer program run by the United States government. The stated mission of the Peace Corps includes providing technical assistance, helping people outside the United States to understand American culture – **to expose** to tell the true facts about sb./sth. and show them to be illegal, immoral etc.; *etw. aufdecken, jdn. entlarven* – **to make a living** *seinen Lebensunterhalt verdienen* – **obstacle** *Hindernis, Hürde* – **to amend** to change a law, document, etc. slightly in order to correct a mistake or improve it – **complacent** too satisfied with yourself or with a situation, so that you do not feel an exchange is necessary; *selbstgefällig*

a) Listen to Clinton's speech for a first time to get a general impression of the issues she raises. While listening to the speech for a second time, take notes about the following topics:

Young people and their role in society: ______________________

____

____

General problems in Tunisia: ______________________

____

____

Unemployment: ______________________

____

____

American promise of action/help: ______________________

____

____

English Language and its importance in education: ______________________________

____

____

Social media: ______________________________

____

____

Follow-up activity

b) During the third listening, complete your notes and pay attention to Clinton's rhetoric.
Clinton uses a lot of stylistic devices to catch the listeners' attention and puts emphasis on certain issues. Fill in the grid below. There is an example at the beginning.

device	quote	effect ?
antithesis	the future ... uncertain, but what is certain ...	emphasis

c) A trainee handed in her notes on Clinton's speech. Some of her sentences are correct, others are not. Correct those which need correction.

Mrs Clinton said:

1. You belong to a remarkable generation of young people, only here in Tunisia and not in the US.

____

2. Now I realize, being young, you may be sceptical.

____

3. So the global economy is not connecting us more than ever before.

____

4. To paraphrase Steve Jobs, we not only need to think different; we need to think big.

____

5. Tunisia is going to build and organize a Global Youth Jobs Alliance.

____

6. Your new democracy needs all the young and old people.

____

d) Finish the following beginnings of conditional clauses, bearing in mind the contents of the speech.

1. If the dictator had not been so corrupt,

____

2. If the Americans had not worked together with Ben Ali, the Tunisians' scepticism

____

3. If the people of Tunisia show a lot commitment in establishing democracy, the USA

____

4. If democracy worked in Tunisia, other Arab states

____

e) A newspaper had asked its trainees to write an editorial on Clinton's speech. Have a look at the texts below and say which one is better and most likely to be published.

Brian Fisher

Everyone understood that Mrs Clinton is on a good-will tour in Tunisia, but the United States does not support Tunisia, Algeria, Syria, and other nations because they love them or because of human rights, but just for their own interests, especially since the White House wants to improve its image with Muslims around the world after the massacres it has committed in Iraq and Afghanistan.

If America claims to support these people in the name of human rights, it must first repair what it has done in Iraq and Afghanistan and other places, despite the fact that nothing and nobody can fix what has been done.

Mary Baker

While listening to the speech of Hillary Clinton, I could understand her intention of preserving rights and freedoms within a real democratic state in Tunisia, as well as the will to help its people financially, economically, and politically by means of cultural exchange, for instance. It seems as if the leaders of this world wanted Tunisia to be an example to follow or a warning to other countries in the region.

Tunisians want to live respectable lives in peace. However, economic support won't be enough, it's an investment in education, morals, and rights that we need to focus on.

To my mind, ____________'s text ______________________________

____

____

____

____

f) Find the corresponding nouns/adjectives/verbs and fill the grid.

noun	adjective	verb
determination		
	violent	
		to exploit
employment		
		to participate
	empowered	
encouragement		

Audio CD 2, Track 1

13 Hillary Clinton
Remarks on Youth

a) Listen to Clinton's speech for a first time to get a general impression of the issues she raises. While listening to the speech for a second time, take notes about the following topics:

Young people and their role in society:

young people in Tunisia and elsewhere want to build lasting democracies/women and youth empowerment/new technologies and their influences on everyday life

General problems in Tunisia:

TV and Internet create demands: living in prosperity, dignity and freedom, employment

Unemployment:

problem among young people/gap between skills and demands of global market/the young have to move to the cities/the old corrupt systems of patronage are outmoded/technologies and ethics must be combined

American promise of action/help:

youth councils at the embassies/Office of Global Youth Issues in Washington/Global Youth Jobs Alliance/ offering job placement and skills training/expanding English language training/encouraging the use of social networking tools

English language and its importance in education:

the language of commerce and the Internet/globally important

Social media:

skills in social networking have to be improved

Follow-up activity

b) During the third listening, complete your notes and pay attention to Clinton's rhetoric.
Clinton uses a lot of stylistic devices to catch the listeners' attention and puts emphasis on certain issues. Fill in the grid below. There is an example at the beginning.

device	quote	effect?
antithesis	the future … uncertain, but what is certain technologies **shrink** your world but **expand** your horizons	emphasis
anaphora	We know … We have been working … We are now … We fought civil war … We had to amend … We continue …	easily remembered

device	quote	effect?
repetition climax	I am very confident – I am very, very confident that ... Why ... did **change** ... that **change** ... spark **change** across the Arab world?	emphasis
metaphors	a port of entry into the global economy grassroots public governments a recipe for frustration/the youth bulge they stand up against corrupt governments	easy to imagine
enumeration	optimistic, innovative, impatient young people	flattering the young
quotations parallelism	Steve Jobs: we not only need to think different, we need to think big	to have a safe warrantor

c) A trainee handed in her notes on Clinton's speech. Some of her sentences are correct, others are not. Correct those which need correction.

Mrs Clinton said:

1. You belong to a remarkable generation of young people, only here in Tunisia and not in the US.

... people, **not** only here in Tunisia, **but across the world**.

2. Now I realize, being young, you may be sceptical.

o.k.

3. So the global economy is not connecting us more than ever before.

... the global economy is **connecting** us

4. To paraphrase Steve Jobs, we not only need to think different; we need to think big, ...

o.k.

5. Tunisia is going to build and organize a Global Youth Jobs Alliance.

We're going to build/The US is going ...

6. Your new democracy needs all the young and old people.

Your new democracy needs you.

d) Finish the following beginnings of conditional clauses, bearing in mind the contents of the speech.

1. If the dictator had not been so corrupt, the Tunisians would not have started an uprising.

2. If the Americans had not worked together with Ben Ali, the Tunisians' scepticism

would have been less apparent/visible.

3. If the people of Tunisia show a lot commitment in establishing democracy, the USA

will reward them with a lot of measures of support.

4. If democracy worked in Tunisia, other Arab countries

could/would copy their democratic system.

e) A newspaper had asked its trainees to write an editorial on Clinton's speech. Have a look at the texts below and say which one is better and most likely to be published.

To my mind, Miss Baker's text seems better suited for publication as her text is more matter-of-fact than the other one. She has understood the main intentions of Mrs Clinton and combined it with some constructive criticism.

Mr. Fisher's text is really ill-suited as he is rather emotional. His allegations are outspoken and blunt and lack evidence.

f) Find the corresponding nouns/adjectives/verbs and fill the grid.

noun	adjective	verb
determination	determined	to determine to be determined
violation	violent	to violate
exploitation	exploited	to exploit
employment	employed	to employ
participation participant	participating	to participate
empowerment	empowered empowering	to empower
encouragement	encouraged encouraging	to encourage

Students' Book, pp. 119 ff.

14 Christopher Dickey
Kill Zone

The Internet article deals with the tragedy of a 17-year-old boy's family in New York and the consequences of the Americans' obsession with guns.

a) Read the article and the statements below and then find out whether they are correctly quoted from the text, starting in l. 57. Note down the lines you refer to to prove whether the statement is right or wrong. There is an example at the beginning.

		True	False
	Summer is the killing season in American cities. Temperature rises but, no, tempers do not. *... rises and, yes, tempers do, too.*		X ll. 57 f.
1.	Collateral carnage like the slaughter of Tyquran's mother is avoidable.		
2.	In Los Angeles County, with an estimated 450 gangs that have 45,000 members, about half the murders are gang related.		
3.	In Chicago, gang and gun violence is restricted to certain parts of the city, ...		
4.	... the first weekend in June, 26 people were shot and seven of them killed.		
5.	... in parts of the city where guns are a way of life ...		
6.	The embattled streets of the city and the gunland of the heartland are wildly different places and the successful attempt to understand the difference ...		

Follow-up activity

b) As their homework, two students handed in the following summaries of the beginning of the text (ll. 1–56). Which one do you think is better? Say why.

Chris
Tyquran Horton is 17 years old and lives in New York, Brownsville, which is pretty dangerous because of gangs and criminals and their love of guns. Two uncles and his mother got shot during the last 21 years. He is not happy and often scared to death about being stopped and searched by the police, as he thinks they do it because of racism. Tyquran has set his mind on going to college and that is why he is studying hard. He often takes comfort from his mother's photo on the wall. He wants to get to the bottom of the American gun madness.

Sophie
Dickey starts off his article on the American gun obsession with a human interest story about Tyquran Horton (17) living in a violent district of NY. In 21 years, two uncles and his mother have been shot.
He has repeatedly been stopped and searched – for no other reason than the colour of his skin – by plain clothes policemen, who have scared him to death. He studies hard and wants to go to college, but in this dangerous neighbourhood his life is difficult.

To my mind, ___________'s text ______________________________________ because

____

____

____

____

____

____

c) Study the last part of the text (ll. 95–134) and say what you learnt about the reasons why people feel the need to possess weapons in the USA and what you think about it.

____

____

____

____

____

____

____

Students' Book, pp. 119 ff.

14 Christopher Dickey
Kill Zone

a) Read the article and the statements below and then find out whether they are correctly quoted from the text, starting in l. 57. Note down the lines you refer to to prove whether the statement is right or wrong. There is an example at the beginning.

		True	False
1.	Collateral carnage like the slaughter of Tyquran's mother is avoidable. *... inevitable and for many innocents it's inescapable ...*		X ll. 61 f.
2.	In Los Angeles County, with an estimated 450 gangs that have 45,000 members, about half the murders are gang related.	X ll. 64–67	
3.	In Chicago, gang and gun violence is restricted to certain parts of the city, ... *... gun violence is endemic ...*		X ll. 73–75
4.	... the first weekend in June, 26 people were shot and seven of them killed.	X ll. 81–83	
5.	... in parts of the city where guns are a way of life ...	X ll. 85 f.	
6.	The embattled streets of the city and the gunland of the heartland are wildly different places and the successful attempt to understand the difference ... *... places, and the failure to understand that difference ...*		X ll. 91–93

Follow-up activity

b) As their homework, two students handed in the following summaries of the beginning of the text (ll. 1–56). Which one do you think is better? Say why.

To my mind, Sophie's text is better as it sticks to the facts, is written matter-of-factly and provides a good introduction to the topic. Sophie uses formal standard language, hypotaxis and the correct tenses. Chris is more or less retelling Tyquran's story. He gives a lot of facts, too, but introduces emotional aspects (not happy, takes comfort), which should be avoided in a summary. His text does not have an introduction. The sentences are shorter than Sophie's and he does not stick to standard language, but occasionally uses colloquial words (pretty, got shot).

c) Study the last part of the text (ll. 95–134) and say what you learnt about the reasons why people feel the need to possess weapons in the USA and what you think about it.

In my opinion, the situation in the USA seems to be rather bad, as the text shows. Obviously, Americans are mad about guns on the one hand and feel they have a right to be able to defend themselves against criminals on the other hand. A good example of a madman and his obsession with guns is Mayor Bloomberg's attacker, who would rather kill someone than hand in his guns.

Audio CD 2, Track 2

15 Eric Bogosian
subUrbia

Eric Bogosian, an American born actor and writer (*1951), whose parents came from Armenia, became famous because of his plays and his critical and humorous soliloquies on stage.
The scene at hand is taken from the beginning of a play in which three high school friends, who are now in their twenties, are hanging out in front of a convenience store and talking about Nazeer Chaudry, an immigrant from Pakistan, working in that shop.

Schmoans referring to an Austrian word meaning '*Küchenfreund*' – **buffster** is a boy or a girl that is 'buff' – **buff** good looking, fine – **Buffman** American comic super hero – **Oreo** US brand name for cookies

a) First study the text at hand carefully as the actors speak quickly. While reading, try to understand the gist and make notes into the grid below:

Setting: ______

Characters: ______

Subject of discussion: ______

Atmosphere: ______

b) While reading and listening – maybe twice – answer the following questions in note form:

1. Why is Tim a fascist according to Buff? ______

2. Why is Nazeer 'nervous' and has a hard time according to Jeff? ______

3. Why was Nazeer practicing the 'Pledge of Allegiance'? ______

4. When does Jeff make fun of Buff? ______

5. Why does Jeff respect Nazeer? ______

6. Why does Tim hate the third-world countries? ______

7. Why does Jeff not agree to Tim's idea of a one-way ticket for Nazeer? ______

8. Whose fault is it that the Asians are badly off? ____________________

____

9. Why is Jeff rather negative about the future? ____________________

____

Follow-up activity

c) After the second – or third – listening, make a short comment on the following tasks:

1. What is the reason for the characters to use foul language? Give examples and discuss them.

____

____

____

2. Why are Buff Macleod and Jeff Gallagher the least suitable people to complain about immigrants to the USA?

____

____

____

3. Concerning the Asians, who is right, Jeff or Tim?

____

____

____

d) Imagine Tim's sister telling her brother that she is going to have a date with Nazeer. Write down what he would say to her.

Tim to his sister: "____________________

____

____

____

____

e) In the box below you will find some terms which can be matched with the definitions below. There is an example at the beginning.

~~immigrant~~ • racial intolerance • ethnicity • citizenship • population border • integration • migration • asylum • seeker emigration • destination • persecution • naturalization

A person who has come to live permanently in a country that is not his/her own: immigrant

1. The line that divides two areas or countries: ______

2. The act of leaving your own country: ______

3. All the people who live in a particular area, city or country: ______

4. The act of enabling sb. to become accepted as a member of a social group: ______

5. A place that sb. is going or being sent to: ______

6. The act of treating sb. in an unfair/cruel way because of their race, gender, religion or beliefs: ______

7. The movement of large numbers of people from one place to another: ______

8. Being unwilling to accept or tolerate people from other ethnicities: ______

9. The act of making sb. who was not born in a particular country a citizen of the country: ______

10. Connected with a nation, race or people that shares certain cultural traditions: ______

11. The legal right to belong to a particular country: ______

12. A person forced to leave his country, who asks to be allowed to stay in another country: ______

f) Perchance, Tim's father, Jim Mitchum, and Jeff's father, Fred Gallagher, meet at the entrance of their multi-story dwelling. They talk about their sons:

Fred G.: Jeff is in a bad mood all the time. Depression would be the right word. And aggression against anybody and anything goes with it.
Tim M.: That's true for Tim, too. It's awful! He's even worse with his trauma after returning from the air force.
Fred G.: Don't say! Tell me about it!
Tim M.: It gives him nightmares, he cries and wakes us all at night. He came down with his helicopter and saw his mates dying. He is the only survivor.
Fred G.: Oh, gosh! What a catastrophe! This is worse than their hanging around and being without jobs.

Later Gallagher tells his wife about their conversation. Put the above conversation into reported speech and remember to change the tenses. Start like this:

I met Tim's father and told him that Jeff was in a bad mood … ______

______

______

______

______

______

Audio CD 2, Track 2

15 Eric Bogosian
subUrbia

a) First study the text at hand carefully as the actors speak quickly. While reading, try to understand the gist and make notes into the grid below:

Setting: dark house/convenience store/music/three young men

Characters: Tim, Buff, Jeff (Nazeer, backstage)

Subject of discussion: about Nazeer/immigrants/racism/third world countries/poverty

Atmosphere: suspense/sometimes aggressive/bleak/gloomy/hopeless

b) While reading and listening – maybe twice – answer the following questions in note form:

1. Why is Tim a fascist according to Buff?

Shows signs of authoritarian behavior and nationalism/wants to kill Nazeer/bullies his friend around while threatening him in foul language

2. Why is Nazeer 'nervous' and has a hard time according to Jeff?

He knows that Nazeer, a Pakistani, is not yet an American citizen ('Stranger in a strange land'.)

3. Why was Nazeer practicing the 'Pledge of Allegiance'?

In order to get his citizenship, he still has to pass the test, which is also about knowing the Pledge of Allegiance by heart.

4. When does Jeff make fun of Buff?

Buff is making fun of Nazeer by reciting the Pledge, but he makes a mistake when he confounds 'indivisible' with 'invisible', which is very funny. Jeff corrects his mistake.

5. Why does Jeff respect Nazeer?

Jeff does not despise Nazeer – in contrast to Tim – because he comes from a third-world country.

6. Why does Tim hate the third-world countries?

While he was in the air force, he had some bad experiences.

7. Why does Jeff not agree to Tim's idea of a one-way ticket for Nazeer?

He has a right – as a human being – to be treated in a fair way.

8. Whose fault is it that the Asians are badly off?

According to Tim, it is their own fault/According to Jeff, it is the Americans' fault.

9. Why is Jeff rather negative about the future?

Their situation is rather hopeless, no jobs, no money and disasters elsewhere (Iraq, Darfur, Haiti) do not hold promise of any improvement.

Follow-up activity

c) After the second – or third – listening, make a short comment on the following tasks:

1. What is the reason for the characters to use foul language? Give examples and discuss them.

Owing to the fact that they are frustrated with their present situation – no jobs, no money, no future – they are aggressive and insult each other (e.g. moron, fascist etc.) Their frustration finds its expression in words like 'shit', 'shits', 'fuck' and 'fucking', which are frequently used.

2. Why are Buff Macleod and Jeff Gallagher the least suitable people to complain about immigrants to the USA?

Obviously, both boys' families came as immigrants, too, as Macloed is a typical Scottish name and Gallagher an Irish one.

3. Concerning the Asians, who is right, Jeff or Tim?

Neither of them. Tim thinks – because he has been to a lot of places with the air force – that he is an expert and despises all other people and calls them sub-human. Jeff, on the other hand, wants to correct Buff on his knowledge of geography and then assigns Nazeer to India although he is from Pakistan.

d) Imagine Tim's sister telling her brother that she is going to have a date with Nazeer. Write down what he would say to her.

Tim to his sister: What the hell are you doing that for? Do you want to spite me or corner me? No, no! I tell you I won't have a fucking Paki in my family.

Stop crying, o.k.! Alright, I'm calming down. Are you aware, what he is doing that for? Of course not. You are blind and simple-minded. Did he not tell you that he still has to pass his test? If he does not succeed, you are his safety net. A marriage will guarantee him the right to stay here and get a green card. Of course, he will tell you that he loves you, but you should always keep in mind that his permit and citizenship are closer to his heart. You don't believe me? O.k., o.k., just wait and see if I'm right.

e) In the box below you will find some terms which can be matched with the definitions below.

1. The line that divides two areas or countries: *border*

2. The act of leaving your own country: *emigration*

3. All the people who live in a particular area, city or country: *population*

4. The act of enabling sb. to become accepted as a member of a social group: integration

5. A place that sb. is going or being sent to: destination

6. The act of treating sb. in an unfair/cruel way because of their race, gender, religion or beliefs: persecution

7. The movement of large numbers of people from one place to another: migration

8. Being unwilling to accept or tolerate people from other ethnicities: racial intolerance

9. The act of making sb. who was not born in a particular country a citizen of the country: naturalization

10. Connected with a nation, race or people that shares certain cultural traditions: ethnicity

11. The legal right to belong to a particular country: citizenship

12. A person forced to leave his country, who asks to be allowed to stay in another country: asylum seeker

f) Per chance, Tim's father, Jim Mitchum, and Jeff's father, Fred Gallagher, meet at the entrance of their multi-story dwelling. They talk about their sons.
Later Gallagher tells his wife about their conversation. Put the above conversation into reported speech and remember to change the tenses. Start like this:

I met Tim's father and told him that Jeff was in a bad mood … and that depression **would be** the right word and that aggression against anybody and anything **went** with it. Jim M. **agreed** and **said** that **that was** true for Tim, too, and that it **was** awful. He claimed that Tim was even worse with his trauma after returning from the air force. I told him that I **did not/could not** believe it and **asked** him **to tell** me more about it. He **said** it **gave** Tim nightmares, he **cried** and **woke** them up at night. He **had come** down with his helicopter and **had seen** his mates dying. He **is/was** the only survivor. I **called that** a catastrophe and **said** that **was** worse than the boys' hanging around or being without jobs.

Audio CD 2, Track 3

16 David Cameron
Speech on the Government's Immigration Policy

Prime Minister David Cameron is a member of the Conservative Party, which is known for its criticism of the Labour Party's state multiculturalism. In the following extract from a speech Cameron gave in April 2011, he explains the Conservative Party's policy on immigration to Great Britain.

assertion *Einschätzung, Überzeugung* – **substantive** *(fml.)* dealing with important matters – **unalloyed** *(fml.)* pure – **sensible** *vernünftig* – **to be hell-bent on doing sth.** *wild entschlossen sein, etwas zu tun* – **to burnish** *(fml.)* here: to emphasize – **credentials** documents that prove that you are who you claim to be and can therefore be trusted – **to starve sb. off sth.** not to give sth. that is needed – **to extinguish sb./sth.** *jemanden oder etwas auslöschen* – **fair-minded** looking at things and judging in a fair and open way – **immeasurable** *unermesslich* – **to forge sth.** here: to shape sth. – **disjointedness** *Zusammenhangslosigkeit* – **to get to grips with sth.** *etwas in den Griff bekommen* – **to account for sth.** to explain sth. – **persistent** *anhaltend, ausgedehnt* – **vacancy** a job that is available to do – **sober** serious and sensible – **comprehensive** complete – **substantial** *umfangreich* – **to enhance sth.** *steigern, erhöhen* – **to be confident** *zuversichtlich sein*

a) Listen to the beginning of Cameron's speech (part 1) and decide whether the following statements are true or false, and fill in the gaps in the final statement. The first line is an example.

	Cameron says that ...	True	False
	the British voters are worried about the high number of immigrants.	X	
1.	the British voters want the politicians to take action.		
2.	the debate on immigration has always been based on good arguments.		
3.	the last government was successful in dealing with immigration.		
4.	discussions about immigration play into the hands of extremist parties.		
5.	immigration is not a central problem in the UK		

On the whole, Cameron wants ______________ immigration, and not ______________ immigration.

b) Before listening to parts 2–4 of the speech, study the following assignments. While listening, take notes of the correct answers. After the second listening you will have time to complete the answers. The first line is an example.

1. Name at least four sectors that profit from immigrants' contributions:

1. schools ______________
2. ______________
3. ______________
4. ______________

2. The number of people who came to Britain between 1997 and 2009: ______________

3. In what field does the existence of a high number of immigrants place pressures on communities:

____

4. According to Cameron, real integration takes ______________

5. Name two negative experiences people could have had with immigrants:

1. ______________________________

2. ______________________________

6. What is Cameron's political aim concerning immigration into Britain?

____

c) Before listening to the end of Cameron's speech (parts 6 and 7), read the following statements and decide how they could be matched. Then listen to end of his speech and decide whether you were correct. The first statement serves as an example (**1–l**).

> **to account for sth.** to explain sth. – **persistent** *anhaltend, ausgedehnt* – **vacancy** a job that is available to do – **sober** serious and sensible – **comprehensive** complete – **substantial** *umfangreich* – **to enhance sth.** *steigern, erhöhen* – **to be confident** *zuversichtlich sein*

1.	Since 1997 there have been
2.	Foreign born workers hold
3.	Welfare is supporting
4.	There is not
5.	British-born people have been paid
6.	Migrant workers have filled
7.	Cameron's plans are sober
8.	Cameron's plans are comprehensive
9.	Cameron's plans are effective
10.	Cameron plans
11.	Britain will continue
12.	Cameron promises

a)	a high number of British-born people.
b)	because they are good for the economy and education.
c)	to control immigration.
d)	to reduce immigration to less than 100,000 a year.
e)	because they cover both positive and negative aspects of immigration.
f)	because they deal with all possibilities of entering Britain.
g)	75 % of the new jobs.
h)	for years by the welfare system.
i)	to welcome the elites and the persecuted.
j)	a fixed number of jobs.
k)	the gaps in the labour market.
l)	2.5 million more jobs.

1 – l, ______________________________

Audio CD 2, Track 3

16 David Cameron
Speech on the Government's Immigration Policy

a) Listen to the beginning of Cameron's speech (part 1) and decide whether the following statements are true or false, and fill in the gaps in the final statement.

	Cameron says that ...	True	False
1.	the British voters want the politicians to take action.	X	
2.	the debate on immigration has always been based on good arguments.		X
3.	the last government was successful in dealing with immigration.		X
4.	discussions about immigration play into the hands of extremist parties.		X
5.	immigration is not a central problem in the UK.		X

On the whole, Cameron wants ___better___ immigration, and not ___mass___ immigration.

b) Before listening to parts 2–4 of the speech, study the following assignments. While listening, take notes of the correct answers. After the second listening you will have time to complete the answers. The first line is an example.

1. Name at least four sectors that profit from immigrants' contributions:

1. schools
2. hospitals
3. business (entrepreneurs)
4. charities

Also possible: financial services, fashion, food, music

2. The number of people who came to Britain between 1997 and 2009: 2.2 million

3. In what fields does the existence of a high number of immigrants place pressures on communities:

school, housing, health care, social pressures, lack of common experiences

4. According to Cameron, real integration takes ___time___.

5. Name two negative experiences people could have had with immigrants:

1. language difficulties

2. no integration, also: discomfort, no sense of community.

6. What is Cameron's political aim concerning immigration into Britain?

to reduce/control the number of immigrants.

c) Before listening to the end of Cameron's speech (parts 6 and 7), read the following statements and decide how they could be matched. Then listen to end of his speech and decide whether you were correct. The first statement serves as an example (**1–l**).

1.	Since 1997 there have been	**l)**	2.5 million more jobs.
2.	Foreign born workers hold	**g)**	75% of the new jobs.
3.	Welfare is supporting	**a)**	a high number of British-born people.
4.	There is not	**j)**	a fixed number of jobs.
5.	British-born people have been paid	**h)**	for years by the welfare system.
6.	Migrant workers have filled	**k)**	the gaps in the labour market.
7.	Cameron's plans are sober	**e)**	because they cover both positive and negative aspects of immigration
8.	Cameron's plans are comprehensive	**f)**	because they deal with all possibilities of entering Britain
9.	Cameron's plans are effective	**b)**	because they are good for the economy and education.
10.	Cameron plans	**d)**	to reduce immigration to less than 100,000 a year
11.	Britain will continue	**i)**	to welcome the elites and the persecuted.
12.	Cameron promises	**c)**	to control immigration

Students' Book, pp. 153 ff.

17 Sandra Cisneros
No Speak English

The text at hand is an extract from the novel *The House on Mango Street*. Its narrator, 12-year-old Esperanza, describes what is going on in the house opposite her flat in an American suburb. As she is a Hispanic herself, her sympathies and even often her commiseration shine through.

a) Read the text and find out what elements betray a 12-year-old narrator. Fill in the grid. There is an example at the beginning.

element	example from the text	reference
short sentences, almost no hypotaxis	He worked two jobs. He came home late and he left early.	ll. 6 f.

b) Why does Esperanza like Mamacita? Where does it become obvious in the text?

____

____

____

____

____

____

____

____

c) Read the extract from the novel again and then the texts below which are summaries handed in by students and find out which one is better.

John
The Mexican wife of Esperanza's neighbour, who has to work hard to make a living on Mango Street, comes to her husband's new home with their baby. She is terribly obese and that is why some of the neighbours think that she does not leave the flat. But there is another reason too, as she hates English and does not want to learn or speak it. When their son starts to talk, she is horrified that he repeats slogans from an American commercial on TV.

Anne
Her nickname is Mamacita and she arrives from Mexico with her baby to the home of her Mexican husband, who is trying to make a living in the US. She does not seem to be happy there as she is homesick and does not want to learn English. That is why she stays in the house and feels isolated and tells her son not to speak English. She wants a pink house in Mexico, but her husband tells her that they have their home in Mango street now.

To my mind, ____________'s text ______________________________ because

____

____

____

____

____

d) Imagine Mamacita is seeing a therapist/psychologist who keeps a medical file/record in the form of a questionnaire which he uses for his notes. Fill in what you think to be useful to him and write down a reference from the text. There are two examples at the beginning.

topic	example	reference
name/nickname	*Mamacita*	*l. 1, l. 8*
single/married	*married with one baby boy*	*l. 1, l. 5, l. 8, l. 60*
address		
ethnicity		
language		
physical problems		
mental state		
social problems		
tics		
therapy		

Students' Book, pp. 153 ff.

17 Sandra Cisneros
No Speak English

a) Read the text and find out what elements betray a 12-year-old narrator. Fill in the grid. There is an example at the beginning.

element	example from the text	reference
short sentences, almost no hypotaxis	He worked two jobs. He came home late and he left early.	ll. 6 f.
incomplete (anaphoric) sentences	Every day. Huge, enormous, beautiful …	l. 7 ll. 14–16
the same beginning of sentences	He saved … He worked … He came home …	ll. 4–7
repetitions	Push pull. Push, pull Up, up, up the stairs … Home. Home. Home. Speak English. Speak English. No speak English … No speak English, no speak English, … No, no, no …	l. 14 l. 18 l. 43 l. 55 ll. 63–65 l. 65
the type of metaphorical language employed	a foot soft as a rabbit's ear to the little rosebuds of her toes a voice that sounds like a seagull as if he had torn the only skinny thread that kept her alive	l. 10 l. 16 ll. 41 f. ll. 57 f.

b) Why does Esperanza like Mamacita? Where does it become obvious in the text?

Esperanza sympathizes with Mamacita, as she, as a Hispanic, has listened to similar stories told by her relatives. Her father has gone through a comparable trauma (because of his lack of English), eating ham and eggs for three months (ll. 30–34).

Esperanza refuses to call her Mamasota (ll. 2 f.) because she thinks it is mean. She is not taken aback by her obesity; on the contrary, she likes it, as she chooses nice comparisons to describe her (*a foot soft as a rabbit's ear*, l. 10), (*… she boomed. Huge, enormous, beautiful to look at, …*, ll. 14 f.).

Esperanza defends her against evil tongues (*she's too fat …*, l. 22) and comes up with a good explanation (*afraid to speak English*, l. 24). She puts two and two together (*sitting by the window, playing the Spanish radio, listening to all the homesick songs*) and finds out that Mamacita is homesick.

When the little boy sings the American commercial, she thinks that it breaks her heart (l. 60).

She sympathizes strongly with her when she insinuates that Mamacita cries (*… then I think she cries*, l. 49) and she puts herself in her shoes and comments, **I would**, l. 49.

c) Read the extract from the novel and then the texts below which are summaries handed in by students and find out which one is better.

To my mind, John's text is somehow better than Anne's because he has focused on all the key facts. Both make use of reported speech, which is against the rules of a summary, but on the whole it is pretty difficult to write a proper summary of this narrative text.

Anne's summary is not bad because she has a full understanding of the text as her basic approach to interpretation reveals.

d) Imagine Mamacita is seeing a therapist/psychologist who keeps a medical file/record in the form of a questionnaire which he uses for his notes. Fill in what you consider to be useful to him and write down a reference from the text. There are two examples at the beginning.

topic	example	reference
name/nickname	Mamacita	l. 1, l. 8
single/married	married with one baby boy	l. 1, l. 5, l. 8, l. 60
address	a third-floor flat in a house on Mango street	l. 2
ethnicity	Hispanic	whole text
language	Spanish only	ll. 25 f., l. 55, l. 63
physical problems	obesity	l. 3, ll. 12 f., ll. 22 f.
mental state	depression/homesickness/hysterics/ phobia about English	ll. 22–66
social problems	her self-inflicted isolation, lonesomeness unwilling to leave the flat unwilling to learn English unwilling to assimilate	ll. 23 f., ll. 35–39, l. 55 ll. 22–66 almost in the whole text
tics	fixated on the colour pink	l. 10, l. 15, ll. 43–49
therapy	making her talk about her situation making her meet with other women with similar problems	

Film CD-ROM, Track 7

18 Jhumpa Lahiri
The Namesake

The extract at hand – from the novel *The Namesake* by Jhumpa Lahiri – is about a 14-year-old boy, who has been irritated by his strange first name Gogol all his life. His parents, Ashoke and Ashinia Ganguli, both born in India, and Gogol and his younger sister Sonia, live in the USA and are about to celebrate Gogol's birthday.

a) While reading the extract, find out about the father and son and look for the quotes in the grid, classify them by referring them to the person concerned (father or son) and say what the quote reveals about them. There is an example at the beginning.

quote	f. or s.	ref.	significance
For the first time in his life, he has said no to the frosted cake	son	ll. 7 f.	wants to show that he has grown up/no more kindergarten-style parties
but this year ... he has something special			
leans over toward the stereo to turn the volume down a bit.			
"Thanks ... eager to return to his lyrics			
At dinner he sometimes uses a fork			
is still standing in his room, watching expectantly, his hands clasped ...			
wears a Harvard sweatshirt and gray Levi's corduroys			
he could have had an alternative identity			
takes the opportunity to sit beside him on the bed			

quote	f. or s.	ref.	significance
He lifts the book ... running a hand protectively over the cover			
the day ... the memory of his accident has receded			
Today ... is a day to honor life, not brushes with death.			
He fastens the lock on the door knob for good measure.			

b) Why does Gogol's father come into his room?

______

______

______

______

______

______

Follow-up activity

c) In the novel and in the film Ashoke shrinks back from telling Gogol what he wanted to tell him. Why does he do so?

______

______

______

______

______

______

d) In the text, Gogol has got several names: Goggles, Dada, and he would prefer Leo, Anton, Alex or even Nikhil and dreams of "an alternative identity, a B-side to the self", ll. 116 f. Try to unravel this chaos and give an interpretation of the above quote.

e) In comparison with his behaviour in the novel, Gogol is rude to his father in the film version. Give examples and say why the staging of the film had to resort to this change from the original.

f) Study the key words and phrases below – concerning some differences between the written text and the film version – and put them into the grid:

birthday • to shut the door • playing the air guitar • White Album of the Beatles
a small potbelly visible • to open the curtain • graduation • all-colored sweater vest
Ashoke looks slender • black moustache • sitting cross-legged on the bed
moustache turning gray • Pearl Jam CD • clothes: gray shirt, dark trousers

Written text	Film version

Find an explanation – if possible – for some of the differences between the text and film version.

____

____

____

____

____

____

g) What does the text reveal about Gogol's attitude to the Western (American) and Eastern (Indian) cultures and personal habits?

____

____

____

____

____

____

____

____

h) Grammar Exercise: Which tense is the right one: the present, past or past perfect?
Study the text and fill in the gaps. There is an example at the beginning.

In the years 2001 and 2002, Jhumpa Lahiri **wrote** the novel which ____________ **to be published** in 2003. She ________ **to do** a lot of research on the subject in those two years before the first publication. Originally, it ____________ **to be** a novella that ____________ **to be published** in *The New Yorker* and ______________ **to be expanded** later to a full novel.

As she ____________ **to have** problems herself to adjust to two totally different cultures, she ________ **to think** her identity problems ____________ **to be** a daily experience of thousands of people throughout the world. Lahiri ____________________ **not to be surprised**, when in 2005 Mira Nair ________ **to ask** her to allow a film adaptation. A screenplay ____________ **to be written** and for this purpose Mira fortunately ____________ **to recall** her friend Sooni Taraporevala, whom she ____________ **to meet** at Harvard University.

While the story of *The Namesake* ________ **to span** multiple cultures, so ________ **to do** the money backing it. The $10.5 million film ______________________________ **to be co-financed** by the Indian production company UTV Motion Pictures, Fox Searchlight Pictures and the Japanese company Entertainment Farm.

A funny thing about this film ________ **to be** the fact that the main actor Kal Penn ____________ **to be** chosen by Mira Nair's son Zohran. The teenager ____________ **to see** Penn in some comedies and ________ **to make** his mother take Penn on for the film. In the end, everything ____________ **to turn** out well, as the film ____________ **to succeed** at the box office and they ________ **to make** a lot of money, which they ______________________________ **not to expect**.

Film CD-ROM, Track 7

18 Jhumpa Lahiri
The Namesake

a) While reading the extract, find out about the father and son and look for the quotes in the grid, classify them by referring them to the person concerned (father or son) and say what the quote reveals about them. There is an example at the beginning.

quote	f. or s.	ref.	significance
For the first time in his life, he has said no to the frosted cake	son	l. 7 f.	wants to show that he has grown up/no more kindergarten style parties
but this year ... he has something special	father	ll. 48–50	wants to demonstrate commitment, has wrapped it himself, does not give the present his wife has bought
leans over toward the stereo to turn the volume down a bit.	son	l. 63	is being polite to his father, who wants to talk to him
"Thanks ... eager to return to his lyrics	son	ll. 67 f.	gives very short answers, does not want to talk to him, is occupied, but does not tell him bluntly
At dinner he sometimes uses a fork	son	ll. 71 f.	adopts western customs
is still standing in his room, watching expectantly, his hands clasped ...	father	ll. 73 f.	is patient, waiting for his son to show interest
wears a Harvard sweatshirt and gray Levi's corduroys	son	ll. 94–96	does not want to show his Indian background
he could have had an alternative identity	son	ll. 116 f.	does not accept his first name
takes the opportunity to sit beside him on the bed	father	ll. 125 f.	does not want to be chucked out of the room, wants to tell him s.th. important/to impress him
He lifts the book ... running a hand protectively over the cover	father	ll. 141–143	is very fond of Gogol's short stories, wants his son to cherish the book, too

quote	f. or s.	ref.	significance
the day ... the memory of his accident has receded	father	ll. 165 f.	reflects about the connection between his near-death experience and his son's first name
Today ... is a day to honor life, not brushes with death.	father	ll. 172 f.	is reminded of his experience of being close to death but recognizes that this is more a joyous occasion
He fastens the lock on the door knob for good measure.	son	ll. 186 f.	does not want to be disturbed

b) Why does Gogol's father come into his room?

In former times, his wife had bought the presents and his father had not been actively involved in the purchase. For the very first time, Ashoke wants to give a special gift to his son for this special occasion (for his birthday [in the text] and for his graduation [in the film]).

Follow-up activity

c) In the novel and in the film Ashoke shrinks back from telling Gogol what he wanted to tell him. Why does he do so?

Ashoke had wanted to tell him about the interrelation between the choice of Gogol's first name, his preference for this Russian author, Gogol's birth and his own almost fatal accident. But he did not tell him, Ashoke just gave him the book, because he had the impression that this was not the right moment and that Gogol lacked a certain maturity and understanding of his father's emotional life.

d) In the text, Gogol has got several names: Goggles, Dada, and he would prefer Leo, Anton, Alex or even Nikhil and dreams of "an alternative identity, a B-side to the self", l. 116 f. Try to unravel this chaos and give an interpretation of the above quote.

Gogol seems to be quite unhappy about his first name, because it sounds strange to his mates at school and makes him an outsider. ("Gogol sounds ludicrous to his ears, lacking dignity or gravity.") What he would like to be called is one of those short American first names like Leo, Anton or Alex. Typical of a younger teenage sister, making fun of her elder brother and his name, is Sonia's malapropism "Goggles". Although the beginning takes up the first syllable of Gogol and sounds like it to some degree, it is in reality the equipment of a diver to cover his eyes under water (Taucherbrille). She does not use the Bengali (Bengla) name "Dada" (elder brother), which sounds too much like baby talk, and reflects the hierarchy in the family.

Gogol is annoyed ("dismayed") at some failed opportunities to employ a second name for use in kindergarten or at school and he would even have been happy with 'Nikhil', which is strange to some degree as 'Nikhil' is short for 'Nikolai' which is the Russian writer's first name. Gogol wants to tell his father all the time that Gogol is not his favourite author, but his father's. And then he thinks that he would like to have the same opportunity as his parents when entering India: 'an alternative identity, a B-side to the self'. Now it becomes clear again that Gogol sees himself in the middle of an identity crisis while living in the USA where his parents do everything to make him stick to their Bengali culture and habits. The problem is that Gogol's first name is neither rooted in India nor in America but in Russia and that is why we do understand that he is at a loss what to make of his identity. And it seems as if he were not just looking for a B-side, but more for an A-side, as his behaviour and his attitudes show. The Indian classical music remains untouched on the shelf because he is a Beatles fan; he forgets to take off his sneakers in the flat; he uses a fork sometimes. Even his deodorant and Clearasil betray an American teenager.

e) In comparison with his behavior in the novel, Gogol is rude to his father in the film version. Give examples and say why the staging of the film had to resort to this change from the original.

In the film, Gogol takes a far longer time to turn down the music, obviously trying to signal that he does not want to discuss anything with his father. Turning his back on his father most of the time has the aim of showing him that he is not welcome at the moment. Lying down on the bed and yawning shows his boredom and is rude, too. Gogol's grimaces in the film are meant to be negative signs as well and do not appear in the text. All these elements have to do with the omniscient narrator in the novel, who describes Gogol's feelings and thoughts, aspects which cannot be imitated in the film in the same way. Thus, the acting out and gestures have to take over.

f) Study the key words and phrases below – concerning some differences between the written text and the film version – and put them into the grid:

Written text	Film version
birthday a small potbelly visible White Album of the Beatles sitting cross-legged on the bed all-colored sweater vest moustache turning gray to shut the door	graduation Ashoke looks slender Pearl Jam CD playing the air guitar clothes: gray shirt, dark trousers black moustache to open the curtain

Find an explanation – if possible – for some of the difference between the text and film version.

The novel focuses on Gogol's birthday (14), maybe in the early 1980s (Lennon's obituary on the wall, Jimmy Carter is mentioned (president from 1977–1981)), while the film setting seems to be much later as Gogol is older (18–20) after his high school graduation. Maybe the stage director thought an older boy was more able to read and appreciate a book by Gogol.

In the novel Ashoke as an elderly Bengali shows signs of aging (potbelly/gray moustache), but in the film Ashoke must adjust to the youth image Americans idolize. This is also true for clothes: no colours for a serious family man in the USA, the colours belong to his Bengali past.

g) What does the text reveal about Gogol's attitude to the Western (American) and Eastern (Indian) cultures and personal habits?

Gogol comes across as a normal American high school boy, who is fond of British music (in the novel – the Beatles) or keen on American pop music (song by Pearl Jam in the film) as demonstrated by his jumping on his bed and playing the air guitar. Indian music remains untouched on his shelf.

The film still (photo) makes it clear that the Indian tradition is held up by Gogol's mother as she is the only one to be fully dressed in the Indian way, here in the typical Indian sari. She leaves her mark on the house (a pearl curtain bordering Gogol's room in the film) and their food (lamb curry for his birthday – in the novel). Where personal hygiene is concerned, Gogol is not focused on Indian/oriental perfumes as American products can be found in his room (novel – deodorant and Clearasil).

Gogol's birthday presents from his parents are put aside to be given away to his Indian cousins (in the novel). The only present he cares for is that of his American mates. On the whole, one could say that his clothes and habits are American through and through, e.g. using a fork and wearing sneakers, t-shirts, trousers.

Gogol is – to some degree – a representative of a second generation of immigrants who have difficulties doing the splits between their parents' culture and tradition and the new American lifestyle.

h) Grammar exercise: Which tense is the right one: the present, past or past perfect?
Study the text and fill in the gaps. There is an example at the beginning.

In the years 2001 and 2002, Jhumpa Lahiri __wrote__ the novel which __was published__ in 2003. She __had done__ a lot of research on the subject in those two years before the first publication. Originally, it __was__ a novella that __was published__ in *The New Yorker* and __was__ later __expanded__ to a full novel. As she __had__ problems herself in adjusting to two totally different cultures, she __thought__ her identity problems __were__ a daily experience of thousands of people throughout the world. Lahiri __was not surprised__, when in 2005 Mira Nair __asked__ her to allow a film adaptation. A screenplay __had to be written__ and for this purpose Mira fortunately __recalled__ her friend Sooni Taraporevala, whom she __had met__ at Harvard University.

While the story of *The Namesake* __spans__ multiple cultures, so __does__ the money backing it. The $10.5 million film __is/was co-financed__ by the Indian production company UTV Motion Pictures, Fox Searchlight Pictures and the Japanese company Entertainment Farm.

A funny thing about this film __is__ the fact that the main actor Kal Penn __was/had been chosen__ by Mira Nair's son Zohran. The teenager __had seen__ Penn in some comedies and __made__ his mother take on Penn for the film. In the end, everything __turned__ out well, as the film __succeeded__ at the box office and they __made__ a lot of money, which they __had not expected__.

Students' Book, pp. 175 ff.

19

Clemens Höges

The Children of Sodom and Gomorrah – How Europe's Discarded Computers Are Poisoning Africa's Kids

Read the text and then check the statements below. If the statement is wrong, make corrections in note form. Note down the lines you refer to in order to prove whether the statement is true or false. There is one example given.

		True	False
	People in the West throw away old computers, which all end up being recycled. (Hundreds of thousands of them end up in Africa.)		X (ll. 1–3)
1.	Old PCs and electronics are being disposed of in Africa, but their toxic elements poison African children.		
2.	Children put fire to the PCs to have some fun.		
3.	Bismarck is one of the boys trying to make a living by collecting copper and aluminium.		
4.	The burning computers and their plastic material emit carcinogenic fumes, which the children breathe in.		
5.	The Basel Convention allows developed countries to dispose of their waste in less developed countries.		
6.	The Basel Convention has been signed by many nations, but not by Haiti, Afghanistan and the USA which produces most of the waste.		
7.	Although the waste disposal laws in Germany are very strict, lots of German export firms make big money by bypassing them.		
8.	There is no exploitation or hierarchy among the youngsters on the dumping ground.		
9.	Greenpeace England collected samples from that dump, but the tests proved that they were not toxic.		
10.	Lead is a dangerous substance and causes – if breathed in – a decrease in the size of children's brains and in their intelligence.		
11.	Ghana's Environmental Protection Agency seems to be helpless, as the junk arriving does not stop and as there is no direct proof of the effects of toxins on youngsters. The responsible Chemicals Control director does not have the arguments to stop the influx.		

Students' Book, pp. 175 ff.

19 Clemens Höges

The Children of Sodom and Gomorrah – How Europe's Discarded Computers Are Poisoning Africa's Kids

		True	False
1.	Old PCs and electronics are being disposed of in Africa, but their toxic elements poison African children.	X (ll. 1–5) (ll. 54–58)	
2.	Children put fire to the PCs to have some fun. *(… where children try to eke out a living by selling the scrap.)*		X (ll. 3–5)
3.	Bismarck is one of the boys trying to make a living by collecting copper and aluminium.	X (ll. 30–50)	
4.	The burning computers and their plastic material emit carcinogenic fumes, which the children breathe in.	X (ll. 54–57)	
5.	The Basel Convention allows developed countries to dispose of their waste in less developed countries. *(… forbidding developed countries from carrying out unauthorized dumping of computer waste in less developed countries.)*		X (ll. 65–68)
6.	The Basel Convention has been signed by many nations, but not by Haiti, Afghanistan and the USA which produces most of the waste.	X (ll. 68–73)	
7.	Although the waste disposal laws in Germany are very strict, lots of German export firms make big money by bypassing them.	X (ll. 78–94)	
8.	There is no exploitation or hierarchy among the youngsters on the dumping ground. *(There's a hierarchy, … The young men, … control the big junk scales … sell it to a foundry …)*		X (ll. 99–110)
9.	Greenpeace England collected samples from that dump, but the tests proved that they were not toxic. *(He took samples from mud … ash and soil … He found high concentration of lead, cadmium and arsenic …)*		X (ll. 134–145)
10.	Lead is a dangerous substance and causes – if breathed in – a decrease in the size of children's brains and in their intelligence.	X (ll. 146–151)	
11.	Ghana's Environmental Protection Agency seems to be helpless, as the junk arriving does not stop and as there is no direct proof of the effects of toxins on youngsters. The responsible Chemicals Control director does not have the arguments to stop the influx.	X (ll. 158–161) (ll. 175–179) (ll. 180–184)	

Audio CD 2, Track 7

20 Malala Yousafzai
Speech at the United Nations

Listen to the speech for a first time and get a general understanding of what Malala Yousafzai is talking about. Do not panic if you do not understand some words, try to get the meaning from the surrounding words.
Malala Yousafzai (*1997 in Pakistan) is a schoolgirl who had openly demanded education for girls, which is being denied by the Taliban in her country. In October 2012, together with other girls she was shot in the head. After an intensive course of treatment and a long period of rehabilitation in England, she was fully restored and was given the opportunity to deliver a speech at the UN on her 16th birthday on July 12, 2013.

*__beneficent__ *wohltätig* – *__UAE__ *(abbr.)* United Arab Emirates, a federation of seven emirates – *__to achieve sth.__ to accomplish sth. – *__revenge__ *Rache* – *__compassion__ *Mitgefühl* – *__legacy__ *Erbe, Vermächtnis* – *__to inherit__ *etw. erben* – *__Muhammad Ali Jinnah__ (1878–1948) leader of the All-India Muslim League and founder of Pakistan – *__Bacha Khan__ (1890–1988) independence activist of Pashtun descent, known for his non-violent opposition to the British rule in India – *__Mother Teresa__ (1910–1997) Albanian-born, Roman Catholic religious sister who founded the Missionaries of Charity in India – *__FATA__ *(abbr.)* Federally Administered Tribal Areas, a semi-autonomous region in northwestern Pakistan – *__to blast__ to shoot – *__Pashtun__ people known as ethnic Afghans – *__deprivation__ *Entzug, Verlust, Entbehrung* – *__prosperity__ *Wohlstand* – *__compulsory__ *verpflichtend* – *__creed__ religious belief – *__destination__ goal – *__to shield__ to protect – *__illiteracy__ *Analphabetentum*

a) Listen to Malala's speech for a first time to get a general impression of the issues she raises. While listening to the speech for a second time, take notes about the following topics:

Addressing/thanking people: ______________________________

____

____

Talking about human rights: ______________________________

____

____

Her life-threatening experience and what it taught her: ______________________________

____

____

The Taliban's reason for killing women: ______________________________

____

____

On extremism and its effects on people: ______________________________

____

____

On women's rights/girls' education: ______________________________

____

____

Demanding action from: ______________________________

____

____

Demand for action in other domains/areas: ______________________________

____

____

b) A trainee handed in her notes on Malala's speech. Some of her sentences are wrong, others are not. Correct those which need correction.

1. Malala Yousufzai, a 15-year-old girl from India, spoke at the UN in Washington.

____

2. She had been shot in the head by terrorists and had survived because of a life-saving operation in Great Britain.

____

3. Malala reported about her being attacked by the Taliban and her feelings of revenge.

____

4. It is above all the inequality of women and girls that infuriates her.

____

5. She is appealing to the world to improve the conditions for girls and women.

____

6. Malala asks for schools to abolish illiteracy worldwide, but she forgets about child labour and forced marriages.

____

Follow-up activity

c) A newspaper had asked its trainees to write an evaluation of Malala's speech. Have a look at the texts below and say which one is better and most likely to be published.

Peter Brown:
At the end of her speech, there was a standing ovation as everyone was happy about such a marvellous speech by such a young girl, who performed extraordinarily well in front of such a big crowd, with all the TV cameras on her.
Malala concentrated her demands on better conditions for women and girls who are not treated equally and are prone to abuse (child labour and forced marriages). She put special emphasis on her demand for education for all children is in the fight to overcome illiteracy.

Sue Smith:
Malala Yousafzai, who was shot in the head in October in Swat Valley, Pakistan, by the Taliban, delivered an astonishing speech at the UN, demanding peace and an education for all. She also addressed other global problems as poverty, illiteracy and terrorism.
Unfortunately, only two channels showed her speech live in Pakistan, although she is looked upon as a hero by many Pakistanis, especially by those who oppose the Taliban's campaign of terror and violence.

In my opinion, ___________'s text ____

____

____

____

____

____

____

d) Malala's speech is full of stylistic devices. Write down those figures of speech that struck you most. After having listened to the speech a third time, fill in quotes illustrating the respective stylistic devices. There is an example at the beginning.

stylistic device	quote/reference	effect on the audience
anaphora	*Their right to live in peace. Their right to be …*	*easy to remember*

e) Shortly after her speech, Malala received a letter from a leading Taliban, in which he somehow excused himself for their attempt to kill her, but tried to explain why they wanted to kill her. He argued that it was not because of her demand for education but because of her maligning (*jdn. verleumnden*) the Taliban.
Write a short comment for a newspaper.

To my mind, ______

Audio CD 2, Track 7

20 Malala Yousafzai
Speech at the United Nations

a) Listen to Malala's speech for a first time to get a general impression of the issues she raises. While listening to the speech for a second time, take notes about the following topics:

Addressing/thanking some people: members of the UN (elders), some guests of honour: Ban Ki-moon (UN Secretary), Gordon Brown (former British PM), young spectators (dear brothers and sisters); Thanking all medical staff who were involved in her recovery

Talking about human rights: Malala Day should not be 'her' day but rather one for all human rights activists, as she speaks for all who demand peace, human dignity, equality of opportunity and education.

Her life-threatening experience and what it has taught her: describes the Taliban attack, does not want to give in to terrorism and rejects hate or revenge; quotes some of her idols who stand for compassion and forgiveness

The Taliban's reason for killing women: they are afraid of books and pens/the power of education and the voices of women

On extremism and its effects on people: the Taliban have killed women/girls and blown up schools to show that they are against equality. They are misusing the name of Islam

On women's rights/girls' education: peace is necessary for education, children cannot go to school; child labour in India; Nigeria and Afghanistan are under attack from extremists; forced marriages of young girls; men and women suffer from poverty, ignorance, injustice, racism, deprivation; appeals to women to speak up and to fight for themselves

Demanding action from: world leaders/governments, developed nations, communities – to support and protect women's rights, education for all children: to fight terrorism and violence; to reject prejudice based on caste, creed, sect, religion or gender; to ensure freedom and equality for women

Demand for action in other domains/areas: speaking up in favour of a global struggle against illiteracy, poverty and terrorism by picking up our books and pens

b) A trainee handed in her notes on Malala's speech. Some of her sentences are wrong, others are not. Correct those which need correction.

1. Malala Yousufzai, a 15-year-old girl from India, spoke at the UN in Washington.

   Malala, a 16-year-old girl from Pakistan, spoke at the UN in New York.

2. She had been shot in the head by terrorists and had survived because of a life-saving operation in Great Britain.

o.k.

3. Malala reported about her being attacked by the Taliban and her feelings of revenge.

She said that she did not want to take revenge.

4. It is above all the inequality of women and girls that infuriates her.

o.k.

5. She is appealing to the world to improve the conditions for girls and women.

o.k.

6. Malala calls upon schools to abolish illiteracy worldwide, but she forgets about child labour and forced marriages.

She does not forget to remind the audience of child labour (twice) and forced marriages.

Follow-up activity

c) A newspaper had asked its trainees to write an evaluation of Malala's speech. Have a look at the texts below and say which one is better and most likely to be published.

In my opinion, both texts are not bad, but could both be improved in some respects. The start of Mr. Brown's contribution is centered on the end of the speech and the reaction of the audience. The reader is left to guess who he is speaking about as he does not mention Malala's name nor the occasion. In this respect, Miss Smith's text is far better because she does not turn the event upside down and did some research on the coverage and evaluation of Malala and her speech in her home country.

I like the second part of Mr. Brown's text better than the beginning of Miss Smith's, as he did a good summary of the essentials, while Miss Smith has missed out on Malala's commitment for women's and girls' rights.

Thus, I would not publish either of them.

d) Malala's speech is full of stylistic devices. Write down those figures of speech that struck you most. After having listened to the speech a third time, fill in quotes illustrating the respective stylistic device. There is an example at the beginning.

stylistic device	quote/reference	effect on the audience
anaphora	Their right to live in peace. Their right to be ... We must not forget ... We must not forget ... We call upon all governments ... We call upon ...	easy to remember, asking for attention
antithesis	The thought that the bullet would silence us. But they failed. Weakness, fear and hopelessness died. Strength, power and courage was born. the importance of light when we see darkness	to raise emotions
repetitions	I am the same Malala. My ambitions are the same. My hopes are the same. My dreams are the same. Dear sisters and brothers, re realise ... We realise ... we realised ... And that is why ... And that is why ... And that is why	more effective
a trio of trilogies	Muhammad, Jesus, Buddha ... [...] M.L. King, Mandela, M. Ali Jinnah ... Gandhi, Bacha Khan, Mother Teresa	easily remembered
parallelism climax	There was a time when ... But, this time, we ... now it's time to speak up	reminding all of M. L. King
metaphors	Empower ourselves with the weapon of knowledge and let us shield ourselves with unity The pen is mightier than [the] sword. So let us wage a global struggle against illiteracy, poverty ... let us pick our books ...	to spur on imagination and commitment
parallelism	One child, one teacher, one pen and one book can change the world.	emphasis

e) Shortly after her speech, Malala received a letter from a leading Taliban, in which he somehow excused himself for their attempt to kill her, but tried to explain why they wanted to kill her. He argued that it was not because of her demand for education but because of her maligning the Taliban.
Write a short comment for a newspaper.

In this case there is no need to think twice. Against the background of the events – here the bloody attack on Malala – every student will condemn the Taliban's statement.

An example:

To my mind, this is really unbelievable. How can he excuse his group of murderers on the one hand and justify their action on the other hand?! Not very logical. And what is even more strange is his kind of argument: maligning the Taliban, that was his reproach. I could tell him that they are doing that themselves: a bunch of thugs on a killing spree – one cannot malign them, they are totally evil – even the worst is not bad enough to describe them.

Students' Book, pp. 187 ff.

21 HOKISA – Homes for Kids in South Africa

Read the report *HOKISA – Homes for Kids in South Africa* taken from a book by Lutz van Dijk and then decide whether the statements below are true or false. Tick the appropriate box and indicate the lines where you found the relevant information. Make corrections to the false statements in note form.

		True	False
	HOKISA is a project in South America. HOKISA is a pilot project … South Africa. (introduction)		X
1.	HOKISA is a normal clinic treating children.		
2.	Sive Maholwana was raised in Johannesburg.		
3.	The name of the township is Masiphumelele, which means "We will make it."		
4.	Many people rob tourists.		
5.	"Tsotsis" is a word for rich tourists.		
6.	There are twenty pupils in Sive's class.		
7.	Sive likes to ask questions.		
8.	Sive hasn't got a father.		
9.	Sive wants to know whether he will be gay someday.		
10.	Ayakha and Sive are the best of friends.		
11.	Sive doesn't like Ayakha because he does not have any imagination.		
12.	Grandpa Lutz is Sive's real grandpa.		

Students' Book, pp. 187 ff.

21 HOKISA – Homes for Kids in South Africa

		True	False
1.	HOKISA is a normal clinic treating children. HOKISA … day care clinic … to children affected by HIV/Aids (introduction)		X
2.	Sive Maholwana was raised in Johannesburg. was raised in a township … in a part of **Cape Town**. ll. 18–22		X
3.	The name of the township is Masiphumelele, which means "We will make it." ll. 26–29	X	
4.	Many people rob tourists. Many people are poor … that doesn't mean our parents rob tourists. ll. 39–41		X
5.	"Tsotsis" is a word for rich tourists. … there are some criminals here … called Tsotsis. ll. 42 f.		X
6.	There are twenty pupils in Sive's class. … there are more than fifty … … eighty kids … ll. 63–66		X
7.	Sive likes to ask questions. That's how wonderful it can be if you ask questions. ll. 90 f.	X	
8.	Sive hasn't got a father. … if I knew my father, l. 89; Perry, my HOKISA-Dad, l. 92	X	
9.	Sive wants to know whether he will be gay someday. I asked him: Will I be gay someday … ll. 102 f.	X	
10.	Ayakha and Sive are the best of friends. Ayakha and I are **not** the best of friends. l. 82		X
11.	Sive doesn't like Ayakha because he does not have any imagination. What I don't really like about A. … He just doesn't have any imagination. ll. 83–86	X	
12.	Grandpa Lutz is Sive's real grandpa. Ayakha … his adopted grandpa Lutz … ll. 111–115		X

Audio CD 2, Track 8

22 Made in Germany: Eco-Fashion – Save the Planet and Look Good

Listen to this internet report. Answer the questions in note form. Do not write full sentences. You will hear the recording twice. First look at the questions. After the second listening, complete your notes. At the beginning, there is an example.

run-of-the-mill here: mass-produced, like others

Where does the report come from?

Berlin, the German capital

1. Mrs Winkler, the first shop owner, sells fashion with what kind of background?

2. What is the next shopper's first key idea when buying clothes?

3. What was the trend at the premium fashion trade fair?

4. The label Kuyichi has other priorities? Which are they?

5. According to Kuyichi's, the customers are more critical How has this come about?

6. How does the organization 'Made-By' want to change the image of fashion?

7. What is the advantage of a label with a code sewn into every article of clothing?

8. Why does 'Made-by' seem to be becoming a success?

Audio CD 2, Track 8

22 Made in Germany: Eco-Fashion – Save the Planet and Look Good

1. Mrs Winkler, the first shop owner, sells fashion with what kind of background?

it is an environmentally-friendly fair trade production, with a green label.

2. What is the shopper's first key idea when buying clothes?

the design, the look, no mass-production

3. What was the trend at the premium fashion trade fair?

eco-friendly fashion, but not only green credentials.

4. The label Kuyichi has other priorities? Which are they?

it should look fantastic, style-conscious, organic, fair trade

5. According to Kuyichi's, the customers are more critical How has this come about?

know more about it, show more individual choice, have a changing conscience

6. How does the organization 'Made-By' want to change the image of fashion?

wants to stop spraying pesticides on cotton fields, to improve conditions in textile mills, by means of a good practice certificate

7. What is the advantage of a label with a code sewn into every article of clothing?

chain of production (from the farm to sewing to workshop to store) can be followed by means of the code on the homepage

8. Why does 'Made-by' seem to be becoming a success?

although having started only recently, 24 companies have joined, including Karstadt.

Students' Book, pp. 204 ff.

23 Brita Belli
The Eco-Fashion Revolution: You Are What You Wear

Read the text and then check the statements below. If the statement is wrong, make corrections in note form. Note down the lines you refer to in order to prove whether the statement is true or false. One example is given.

		True	False
	Quite a few eco-designers are involved in giving old things a new appearance.	X (ll. 1–3)	
1.	Some designers do not want their customers to think about the production of their clothes.		
2.	African cotton farmers are using new pesticides that won't harm humans.		
3.	Although eco-fashion has slowly become trendy because of some famous labels, the profits involved speak a different language.		
4.	Only a minority of the shoppers buy organic or sustainable clothing.		
5.	Shoppers are concerned about emissions, global warming, toxins and water conservation all at the same time.		
6.	Shoppers are mostly part of the throwaway society.		
7.	Shoppers should be aware of the origin and manufacture of their clothes.		
8.	A change in shoppers' attitudes towards eco-topics has not yet been noticed by 'Edun'.		
9.	Although organic cotton clothing is growing faster than organic food, most consumers are more interested in colour, style and price than in environmentally-friendly fabric.		
10.	Even very big fashion retailers like GAP want to promote environmentally, socially and economically sustainable cotton cultivation around the globe.		
11.	Interesting trends are: sustainably-made fashion and government-regulated labelling.		
12.	The eco-fashion sector is interested in influencing the consumer's disposable mentality.		

Students' Book, pp. 204 ff.

23 Brita Belli
The Eco-Fashion Revolution: You Are What You Wear

		True	False
1.	Some designers do not want their customers to think about the production of their clothes. *(The designers want their customers to think about the cotton in their clothing … produced.)*		X (ll. 9 f.)
2.	African cotton farmers are using new pesticides that won't harm humans. *("are using expired pesticides – grave negative health effects")*		X (ll. 14 f.)
3.	Although eco-fashion has slowly become trendy because of some famous labels, the profits involved speak a different language.	X (ll. 21–28)	
4.	Only a minority of the shoppers buy organic or sustainable clothing.	X (ll. 30–32)	
5.	Shoppers are concerned about emissions, global warming, toxins and water conservation all at the same time. *(… fractured environmentalism, where some people may be concerned with emissions and global warming, but not with toxins …)*		X (ll. 37–40)
6.	Shoppers are mostly part of the throwaway society.	X (ll. 44–46)	
7.	Shoppers should be aware of the origin and manufacture of their clothes.	X (ll. 55–58)	
8.	A change in shoppers' attitudes towards eco-topics has not yet been noticed by 'Edun'.		X (ll. 59 f.)
9.	Although organic cotton clothing is growing faster than organic food, most consumers are more interested in colour, style and price than in environmentally-friendly fabric.	X (ll. 66–80)	
10.	Even very big fashion retailers like GAP want to promote environmentally, socially and economically sustainable cotton cultivation around the globe.	X (ll. 86–90)	
11.	Interesting trends are: sustainably-made fashion and government-regulated labelling.	X (ll. 100–109)	
12.	The eco-fashion sector is interested in influencing the consumer's disposable mentality. *(The eco-fashion movement … moving away from a disposable mentality.)*	X (ll. 112–115)	

Students' Book, pp. 212 ff.

24 Matt Richtel
Wasting Time Is New Divide in Digital Era

Matt Richtel, born in 1966 in Los Angeles, is a writer and journalist for the *New York Times*, who was awarded the 2010 Pulitzer Prize for National Reporting for a series of articles on the dangerous and harmful use of mobiles, computers and other devices while driving cars. In 2010, Richtel wrote about the impact on the human brain of living with "a deluge of data" from digital devices. He predicted in his investigation that "the way kids' brains ... are developing" is different form their parents and others of older generations.
The article at hand has also been used in a test for students in a foreign language competition in 2013 (*Bundeswettbewerb Fremdsprachen*).

a) Read the online article from the *New York Times* (May 30, 2012) and study the statements below. Tick off (x) the correct continuation, and give the reference from the text. There may sometimes be more than one correct answer. There is an example at the beginning.

statement	**line/ reference**
The "digital divide" ... ☐ **a)** defines the rich only in terms of their use of PCs and other digital devices. ☐ **b)** is mainly about gadgets used for watching shows and videos. ☒ **c)** describes the fact that the world can be divided into people who do and people who don't have access to or can use digital devices.	ll. 1 f.
1. The time-wasting gap ... ☐ **a)** is more a reflection of the ability of the parents to monitor and limit their children's use of technology. ☐ **b)** is mainly an anti-technology tendency on the part of the parents. ☐ **c)** emphasizes the value of putting a computer in every home.	
2. The digital literacy corps ... ☐ **a)** is financially supported by Connect3Compete. ☐ **b)** concentrates mainly on the support of Latin American citizens. ☐ **c)** will be sending thousands of trainers to schools and other institutions to teach people how to use computers.	
3. Digital literacy is important ... ☐ **a)** and will eliminate the digital divide in the USA. ☐ **b)** but broadband access is vital, too. ☐ **c)** as it provides parents and students with the tools and know-how to use PCs for education and job-skills training.	
4. The Kaiser Family Foundation found out ... ☐ **a)** more about the influence of entertainment in connection with the digital divide. ☐ **b)** that children of less-educated parents spend far more time exposed to the media. ☐ **c)** that children are more interested in being entertained than educated by the media.	

statement	**line/ reference**
5. Markiy Cook (12) ... ☐ **a)** is a pupil who prefers doing his homework to games and social networking. ☐ **b)** wants to become a biologist and his grades at school are good. ☐ **c)** stays up all night playing on the weekends and is rather tired on Monday.	
6. Alejandro Zamora (13) ☐ **a)** is addicted to the internet and Facebook, but does not use it for homework. ☐ **b)** whose mother is not afraid of his anger, broke his PC. ☐ **c)** tries to outsmart his mother, who does not know much about computers.	
7. The Ross family ... ☐ **a)** is proud to announce they stick to certain rules while using the internet. ☐ **b)** had a bad experience when one of their grandsons had free access to Edna's PC ☐ **c)** is generally convinced that children need guidance in order to prevent computer mischief.	

Follow-up activity

b) Imagine you are Markiy's teacher talking to him about his last test and his bad mark/grade and questioning him about the hours he spends on the computer and his sleepiness on Mondays.
Against the background of the text, write a dialogue. What advice does the teacher give him?

Teacher: Hello, Markiy, tell me, did your mark go down well with your parents?
Markiy: ______________________________

____

____

____

____

____

____

c) The following words and expressions are all to do with the media. How could you group them? Think of two or three headlines and find out to which group each word belongs. Some words could belong to more than one group.

digital literacy • to speak to s.b. • headline • broadband • to telephone • addressee • to access the Internet • chat room • digital divide • to text • to share • email • copy • literacy • cover story • banner • to delete • community • to publish a newspaper • website • editorial • to cover a subject • to surf • to click on a link • to communicate • to appeal to s.o. • advert • to connect with s.b. • letter to the editor • to entertain • to address sth.

print media	electronic media	personal media

d) Imagine you had to decide which of the following comments on Richtel's articles were to be published. Choose one of them and say why.

Roxy

This article is somehow misleading as it makes it sound like the poor group is doing substantially worse when they are not. Both groups are spending a large amount of time using media for entertainment. It's a difference of roughly 90 minutes, yet judging from the comments the low income group gets most of the blame.
This type of reporting does nothing but evoke stereotypes and negative views towards low-income groups, which in this article also corresponded to minorities.

Tina

The article's main point is that young people are spending too much time using screens, including television and computers. In addition, with the increased availability and affordability of computers and online access, low-income children are spending more time online for entertainment instead of education than middle and higher-income kids.
I wonder if they may be making a mountain out of a molehill. The statistics provided painted an alarming picture of the increase in time spent in front of a screen from 1999 to the present but do not seem to me to be very reliable. If someone was watching TV and surfing the Web at the same time for the same one hour, they would count that as two hours.

To my mind, ____________'s comments ____

____

____

____

____

____

____

e) Imagine you are a journalist giving a press review on TV, in which you talk about Richtel's article from the *New York Times*, highlighting some key sentences. Read the following quotes from the article and change them into reported speech. There is an example at the beginning.

The term "digital divide" emerged to describe technology's haves and have-nots.

Richtel wrote that the term "digital divide" had emerged to describe technology's haves and have-nots.

1. As access to devices has spread, children in poorer families are spending considerably more time using their television ...

____

____

____

2. The new divide is such a cause of concern ...

____

____

3. The commission will help send digital literacy trainers this fall ...

____

____

4. Some of the financial support comes from private companies ...

____

____

5. Instead of closing the achievement gap, they are widening the time-wasting gap.

____

____

6. She got a Hewlett-Packard computer last year through a project funded by the National Institutes of Health ...

____

____

Students' Book, pp. 212 ff.

24 Matt Richtel
Wasting Time Is New Divide in Digital Era

a) Read the online article from the *New York Times* (May 30, 2012) and study the statements below. Tick off ☒ the correct continuation, and give the reference from the text. There may sometimes be more than one correct answer. There is an example at the beginning.

statement	line/ reference
The "digital divide" ...	
☐ **a)** defines the rich only in terms of their use of PCs and other digital devices.	
☐ **b)** is mainly about gadgets used for watching shows and videos.	
☒ **c)** describes the fact that the world can be divided into people who do and people who don't have access to or can use digital devices.	ll. 1 f.
1. The time-wasting gap ...	
☒ **a)** is more a reflection of the ability of the parents to monitor and limit their children's use of technology.	ll. 15–18
☐ **b)** is mainly an anti-technology tendency on the part of the parents.	
☐ **c)** emphasizes the value of putting a computer in every home.	
2. The digital literacy corps ...	
☐ **a)** is financially supported by Connect3Compete.	
☐ **b)** concentrates mainly on the support of Latin American citizens.	
☒ **c)** will be sending thousands of trainers to schools and other institutions to teach people how to use computers.	ll. 29–32
3. Digital literacy is important ...	
☐ **a)** and will eliminate the digital divide in the USA.	
☒ **b)** but broadband access is vital, too.	ll. 46–49
☒ **c)** as it provides parents and students with the tools and know-how to use PCs for education and job-skills training.	ll. 48–53
4. The Kaiser Family Foundation found out ...	
☒ **a)** more about the influence of entertainment in connection with the digital divide.	ll. 80–82, 89–95
☒ **b)** that children of less-educated parents spend far more time exposed to the media.	ll. 69–88
☒ **c)** that children are more interested in being entertained than educated by the media.	ll. 89–95
5. Markiy Cook (12) ...	
☐ **a)** is a pupil who prefers doing his homework to games and social networking.	
☐ **b)** wants to become a biologist and his grades at school are good.	
☒ **c)** stays up all night playing on the weekends and is rather tired on Monday.	ll. 107–110

statement	line/ reference
6. Alejandro Zamora (13)	
☒ **a)** is addicted to the internet and Facebook, but does not use it for homework.	ll. 120–124
☐ **b)** whose mother is not afraid of his anger, broke his PC.	
☐ **c)** tries to outsmart his mother, who does not know much about computers.	
7. The Ross family ...	
☐ **a)** is proud to announce they stick to certain rules while using the internet.	
☒ **b)** had a bad experience when one of their grandsons had free access to Edna's PC	ll. 151–156
☒ **c)** is generally convinced that children need guidance in order to prevent computer mischief.	ll. 142–160

Follow-up activity

b) Imagine you are Markiy's teacher talking to him about his last test and his bad mark/grade and questioning him about the hours he spends, on the computer and his sleepiness on Mondays.
Against the background of the text, write a dialogue. What advice does the teacher give him?

Teacher: Hello, Markiy, tell me, did your mark go down well with your parents?

Markiy: *Gosh! I haven't told them, yet.*

T.: *Why did you not tell them?*

M.: *They might think up some bad countermeasures.*

T.: *What do you mean?*

M.: *O.k. They have warned me about my "intolerable behaviour" as they call it.*

T.: *What would that be?*

M.: *Well, they complain about my being on the internet all the time.*

T.: *Alright, that was what I supposed, too. And what is it precisely?*

M.: *O.k. I can't stop surfing on the internet. Especially, on the weekends, I stay up all night and that is why I am so sleepy on Mondays.*

T.: *Do you want me to talk to your parents?*

M.: *By no means, NO! They will take away my laptop and my playstation.*

T.: *Well, that would be one good step in the right direction. But could you not decide to do that by yourself? If you don't do it now, you will fail in all the subjects and you will be left on the shelf. You are squinching up your face. O.k. Markiy, it's up to you. You HAVE to do something about it NOW or it will be too late. We'll talk about it more tomorrow. Bye.*

c) The following words and expressions are all to do with the media. How could you group them? Think of two or three headlines and then find out to which group each word belongs. Some words could belong to more than one group.

print media	electronic media	personal media
literacy headline addressee cover story banner, copy to communicate letter to the editor advert editorial to cover a subject to publish a newspaper	digital literacy broadband, to appeal to s.o. digital divide access to the Internet, to surf, to text, to share, to delete email, website chat room, community, to communicate, advert, to click on a link to connect with s.b. to entertain, to speak to s.o.	literacy addressee to telephone to communicate to speak to s.o. to appeal to s.o. to address sth.

d) Imagine you had to decide which of the following comments on Richtel's articles were to be published. Choose one of them and say why.

To my mind, Tina's comment is very good, as she did a very good summary in her first paragraph, using excellent language. The second paragraph starts off with a good idiom and metaphor, catching the main ideas in one image. She has a clear opinion and some point of criticism, which makes this text my favourite.

Roxy's text is quite good, too. His or her different points of criticism are well-founded. That is especially true of the last paragraph where Roxy doubts the reliability of the statistics put forward.

If the paper had enough space, I would publish both comments.

e) Imagine you are a journalist giving a press review on TV, in which you talk about Richtel's article from the New York Times, highlighting some key sentences. Read the following quotes from the article and change them into reported speech. There is an example at the beginning.

The term "digital divide" emerged to describe technology's haves and have-nots.

Richtel wrote that the term "digital divide" had emerged to describe technology's haves and have-nots.

1. As access to devices has spread, children in poorer families are spending considerably more time using their television ...

Richtel wrote that children in poorer families were spending more time using their television as access to devices had spread.

2. The new divide is such a cause of concern ...

Richtel wrote that the new divide was such a cause of concern ...

3. The commission will help send digital literacy trainers this fall ...

Richtel wrote that the commission would help send digital literacy trainers that fall ...

4. Some of the financial support comes from private companies ...

Richtel said that some of the financial support came from private companies ...

5. Instead of closing the achievement gap, they are widening the time-wasting gap.

Richtel wrote that they were widening the time-wasting gap, instead of ...

6. She got a Hewlett-Packard computer last year through a project funded by the National Institutes of Health ...

Richtel wrote that the year before she had got a Hewlett-Packard computer through a project funded by the NIH.

Students' Book, pp. 224f.

25 Robert Waugh
TXT BAD 4 UR BRAIN? Text Messaging Can Dent Your Reading Abilities Say Scientists

Read the online article from *The Daily Mail* and tick off the correct answer (a, b, c, or d). Only one answer is correct. At the beginning there is an example.

Text messaging ...

- ☐ is going to reduce your ability to communicate in everyday life.
- ☐ can be a nuisance to others who want to be entertained by the texter.
- ☐ should not interfere with your flexibility and understanding of language.
- ☒ may stunt reading skills, according to new research comparing text users with people who preferred to read newspapers and books.

1. People who read traditional printed language ...

- ☐ generally show more flexibility and understanding of language than texters.
- ☐ enjoy the creativity in language and use it in their daily communication.
- ☐ are annoyed by the slangy form of text messages.
- ☐ are much more comfortable with accepting and understanding new words.

2. While the UK's poet laureate, Carole Ann Duffy, claimed ...

- ☐ that everybody should write a poem now and then, others think differently.
- ☐ that there was no difference between a texter and a normal reader.
- ☐ "The poem is a form of texting".
- ☐ that text messaging did not seem 'creative' on the whole.

3. People who text heavily ...

- ☐ are at a disadvantage compared to those who read a lot.
- ☐ generally use restricted codes and often feel unable to understand uncommon words.
- ☐ could be less able and willing to learn new words.
- ☐ look upon language as an unimportant vehicle of expression or frustration.

4. Textisms ...

- ☐ do not always stand for simple words.
- ☐ represent real words which are commonly known among people who text.
- ☐ abolish "old-fashioned" spelling.
- ☐ do not have any restrictions or linguistic constraints.

Students' Book, pp. 224 f.

25 Robert Waugh
TXT BAD 4 UR BRAIN? Text Messaging Can Dent Your Reading Abilities Say Scientists

1. People who read traditional printed language ...

- [ ] generally show more flexibility and understanding of language than texters.
- [ ] enjoy the creativity in language and use it in their daily communication.
- [ ] are annoyed by the slangy form of text messages.
- [x] are much more comfortable with accepting and understanding new words.

2. While the UK's poet laureate, Carole Ann Duffy, claimed ...

- [ ] that everybody should write a poem now and then, others think differently.
- [ ] that there was no difference between a texter and a normal reader.
- [x] "The poem is a form of texting".
- [ ] that text messaging did not seem 'creative' on the whole.

3. People who text heavily ...

- [ ] are at a disadvantage compared to those who read a lot.
- [ ] generally use restricted codes and often feel unable to understand uncommon words.
- [x] could be less able and willing to learn new words.
- [ ] look upon language as an unimportant vehicle of expression or frustration.

4. Textisms ...

- [ ] do not always stand for simple words.
- [x] represent real words which are commonly known among people who text.
- [ ] abolish "old-fashioned" spelling.
- [ ] do not have any restrictions or linguistic constraints.

Audio CD 2, Track 9

26 Charlie Rose
Exclusive Interview with Facebook Leadership

First study the assignments below before listening to the extract from the interview of Mark Zuckerberg and Sheryl Sandberg, which was chaired by Charlie Rose in November 2011. The part you are listening to is the very beginning of the interview in which Sandberg and Zuckerberg are asked about themselves, their careers, their involvement in Facebook, users' intentions, etc.

Charlie Rose (* 1942) Emmy award winning journalist has been praised as "one of America's premier interviewers" – **Harvard** elite university in Cambridge, Massachusetts – **freshman** a student in his first year of high school, college etc. – **Bill Gates** (* 1955) founder of Microsoft – **Steve Jobs** (1955–2011) founder of Apple – **to drop out** *etw. abbrechen* – **Secretary of the Treasury** *Finanzabteilung* – **to recruit s.o.** to employ s.o. – **to apply sth. to sth.** *etw. auf etw. anwenden* – **valuable** *wertvoll* – **entity** *Einheit* – **lark** *(infml.)* a thing you do for fun or a joke – **to merge with** *sich vermischen mit, ineinander übergehen* – **fabric** structure – **impact** effect – **expansive** growing – **enabler** a person who makes sth. happen or possible – **mind-blowing** *überwältigend* – **dorm room** *Schlafsaal* – **inevitable** *unvermeidlich* – **to figure** *(infml.)* – to think, to imagine – **Spotify** a commercial music streaming service – **MALA** a digital profile including the latest music, songs, etc. – **subscriber** *Abonnent* – **matrix** network – **crowd** here: an anonymous group of people – **to apply to sth.** *sich auf etw. beziehen* – **core** most important, main, essential – **desire** *Begehren* – **periphery** the outer edge of a particular area; *Umfeld*

a) While listening for the first time, try to understand the gist of what is said and then use the following keywords and take short notes:

Careers: ____________________

____

____

Facebook: Z. + S.: ____________________

____

____

Opportunities: ____________________

____

Zuckerberg's intentions/aims while at Harvard: ____________________

____

Social networking: ____________________

____

Users' Intentions: ____________________

____

____

Listen to the interview again to complete your notes.

b) You may listen a third time to the interview and then tick off which of these statements is right. Sometimes more than one answer may be correct.

1. Mark Zuckerberg

☐ a) was a freshman at Cambridge University.

☐ b) worked together with Bill Gates and Steve Jobs.

☐ c) recruited Sheryl from Google.

2. Sheryl Sandberg

☐ a) is a graduate from Harvard University.

☐ b) was portrayed in *Time* magazine as Woman of the Year.

☐ c) is one of the most powerful women in business.

3. Facebook

☐ a) is a social entity almost twice as large as the US.

☐ b) has merged with the social structure of American life.

☐ c) has got half of all Americans as its users.

4. The mission of the company

☐ a) is to improve personal relationships.

☐ b) is to make the world more open and connected.

☐ c) is to sell people music and films.

5. Everything started at university

☐ a) where he met the Winklevoss twins.

☐ b) where they had pizza every night.

☐ c) where they had the idea of creating a community for themselves.

6. Friends are important

☐ a) as they share their views with you.

☐ b) as every single service is now gonna be better with your friends.

☐ c) and staying in touch with them.

7. The wisdom of crowds

☐ a) is represented only in Google.

☐ b) is mostly based on anonymity.

☐ c) consists in the connection between people.

8. The social web

☐ a) did not exist before and can't exist until you are your real self online.

☐ b) was there even before Facebook.

☐ c) is there to satisfy this human desire to communicate.

Follow-up activity

c) Put the following sentences into reported speech by using simple past tense in the main clause. There is an example at the beginning.

1. I want to spend some more time learning from Sheryl.

Zuckerberg said that he wanted to spend some more time learning from Sheryl.

2. I was just really interested because I had a lot of respect.

3. How can I apply some of those things to Facebook?

4. People can stay connected in ways they couldn't before.

5. We thought that there would be something like this.

d) In January 2011 Mark Zuckerberg claimed in an interview that privacy was dead. Against the background of the interview at hand, what do you think about this?

e) The present interview puts a great deal of emphasis on friends and friendship and people Zuckerberg befriended during his time at university, but fact is that with some of them he ended up in the law courts. At least two of them, the Winklevoss twin brothers, sued (*gerichtlich verklagen*) him for having stolen their idea, which became Facebook later on. He paid them $300 million, but still maintained his assertion (*Behauptung*) that he had not deceived them. Comment on this.

Audio CD 2, Track 9

26 Charlie Rose
Exclusive Interview with Facebook Leadership

a) While listening for the first time, try to understand the gist of what is said and then use the following keywords and take short notes:

Careers: Z.: studied at Harvard – Person of the Year – to learn from S. – in less than seven years > network > merging American lives and many lives all over the world; Sandberg worked for Google – S. and Z. are a good fit

Facebook: Z. + S. wanted a total change/new levels of impact and consequence/800 million using Facebook every month/expansive enabler of human communication

Opportunities: the ability given to people to stay in touch/to organize new things/learn about new products or movies or music

Zuckerberg's intentions/aims while at Harvard: to create a cool community/social network/to be the first to create that tool to enable people to connect

Social networking: people signing up for Facebook to stay in touch/800 million/more people use Facebook than Spotify or MALA

Users' Intentions: to find out what your friends prefer/to participate in the social network/wisdom of crowds/information on everything/anything/what does everybody think/to realize the core desire to express oneself

Listen to the interview again to complete your notes.

b) You may listen a third time to the interview and then tick off ☒ which of these statements is right. Sometimes more than one answer may be correct.

1. Mark Zuckerberg

☐ a) was a freshman at Cambridge University.

☐ b) worked together with Bill Gates and Steve Jobs.

☒ c) recruited Sheryl from Google.

2. Sheryl Sandberg

☐ a) is a graduate from Harvard University.

☐ b) was portrayed in Time magazine as Woman of the Year.

☒ c) is one of the most powerful women in business.

3. Facebook

- [x] a) is a social entity almost twice as large as the US.
- [ ] b) has merged with the social structure of American life.
- [ ] c) has got half of all Americans as its users.

4. The mission of the company

- [ ] a) is to improve personal relationships.
- [x] b) is to make the world more open and connected.
- [ ] c) is to sell people music and films.

5. Everything started at university

- [ ] a) where he met the Winklevoss twins.
- [x] b) where they had pizza every night.
- [x] c) where they had the idea of creating a community for themselves.

6. Friends are important

- [ ] a) as they share their views with you.
- [x] b) as every single service is now gonna be better with your friends.
- [x] c) and staying in touch with them.

7. The wisdom of crowds

- [ ] a) is represented only in Google.
- [ ] is mostly based on anonymity.
- [x] c) consists in the connection between people.

8. The social web

- [x] a) did not exist before and can't exist until you are your real self online.
- [ ] b) was there even before Facebook.
- [x] c) is there to satisfy this human desire to communicate.

Follow-up activity

c) Put the following sentences into reported speech by using simple past tense in the main clause. There is an example at the beginning.

1. I want to spend some more time learning from Sheryl.

Zuckerberg said that he wanted to spend some more time learning from Sheryl.

2. I was just really interested because I had a lot of respect.

He said that he had just been interested because he had had a lot of respect.

3. How can I apply some of those things to Facebook?

He wondered/asked himself how he could apply some of these things to Facebook.

4. People can stay connected in ways they couldn't before.

He said that people could stay connected in ways they couldn't/had not been able to before.

5. We thought that there would be something like this.

He said that he had thought that there would be something like that.

d) In January 2011 Mark Zuckerberg claimed in an interview that privacy was dead. Against the background of the interview at hand, what do you think about this?

The answer depends mainly on the general opinion of the student or his/her admiration of idols of IT, which might induce him/her to cover up Zuckerman's negative characteristics. Zuckerberg's main intention is, arguably, not the improvement of friendship but making money by advertising products.

If the student is open-minded, he will have recognized that a major aspect of Facebook is the revelation of private ideas and ways of behaviour, and thus doing away with privacy, as the whole world can see your photos and everything that you reveal on the web.

Zuckerberg's claim that privacy is no longer a social norm is not surprising because anything else would be counterproductive to his own business interests.

Privacy, however is a fundamental human right, which we should not forsake with levity.

e) The present interview puts a great deal of emphasis on friends and friendship and people Zuckerberg befriended during his time at university, but fact is that with some of them he ended up in the law courts. At least two of them, the Winklevoss twin brothers, sued (gerichtlich verklagen) him for having stolen their idea, which became Facebook later on. He paid them $300 million, but still maintained his assertion (Behauptung) that he had not deceived them. Comment on this.

Again (as in d)) the student's general opinion may dominate his/her answer. If the student is open-minded, he/she will recognize that Zuckerberg is cut and dry/callous/insensitive, putting his interests/success/profits above his alleged high opinion on friendship. Zuckerberg at any rate was accused of intentionally misleading his friends and using their ideas to set up his project.

Students' Book, p. 239

27 Rosemary Bennett

Why Facebook Friends Click When They Meet in the Flesh

The present article taken from the science internet page of *The Times* reports on research by Dr. Sam Roberts, whose studies have provided new insights into the dynamics of social relationships. The text at hand focuses on the personal value of social networking.

a) Read the article at hand and then the text below, which is a kind of summary, in which some words have been deleted that can be found in the box below.

lecturer • friends • psychology • Twitter • communication • love • personal contact • interviews • findings • love • difference • Facebook • friendships • social networks

Everyday life shows that talking to your __________________ is not the same as chatting to others on __________________. Research carried out by Dr. Sam Roberts, a senior __________________ in __________________ at the University of Chester, points to the growing number of people chatting to friends on social networks instead of actually meeting them. He had started on the assumption (*Annahme*) that friendships could be more efficiently maintained with the help of the social media. His __________________ indicate the contrary.

Against the background of more than 300 __________________, it has been revealed that people who do not use Facebook very often felt closer to their friends, were happier, and laughed more than those using __________________ a lot.

Interesting, too, was another revelation about active users and simple browsers of social networks in terms of the intensity of their friendships. Roberts found out that there is no __________________ between them. __________________ cannot be replaced by any media, except by Skype, which made people similarly happy.

Follow-up activity

b) Have a look at the following box and then match the nouns with the respective topic:

Twitter • word • smart phone • pinterest • linux • word • instagram • thunderbird • google • mobiles • GPS • cell phone • VK • newspapers • opera • PCs • yahoo • drones • landline phone • TV • yippy • mobiles • meetup • Facebook • open office • firefox • lycos • chrome • bing • google • tumblr

Social networks: Twitter, __________________

Media: __________________

Telephones: __________________

Software programs: __________________

Surveillance: __________________

Search engines: ______________________________

Browser: ______________________________

c) The following sentences in reported speech have to be transformed into direct speech. There is an example at the beginning.

1. Zuckerberg said that he had registered one billion users the month before.

Zuckerberg: I have registered one billion users last month.

2. Roberts asked what results would reveal new insights into friendship that would be published the following week.

____

____

3. Sandberg referred to Zuckerberg, saying that she had always been fond of him and that she was looking forward to working with him on new projects.

____

____

4. Gates said that he had spent billions on health care for African children and that he would even open another relief programme for sufferers of HIV.

____

____

d) Bennett has used some interesting, sometimes metaphorical expressions in her report. Make a list of them and state what they mean. Then select one you like and state why. There is an example at the beginning.

quote	meaning	reference
friends click	friends understand each other immediately and get on well	headline

To my mind, ____

____

____

____

____

____

____

e) Imagine some friends of your 10-year-old brother want to fetch him for a football match, but he does not want to join them because he prefers to stay connected to Facebook at the moment. Against the background of the text, what would you tell him?

____

____

____

____

____

____

____

____

Students' Book, p. 239

27

Rosemary Bennett

Why Facebook Friends Click When They Meet in the Flesh

a) Read the article at hand and then the text below, which is a kind of summary, in which some words have been deleted that can be found in the box below. Complete the text.

Everyday life shows that talking to your friends is not the same as chatting to others on Facebook. Research carried out by Dr. Sam Roberts, a senior lecturer in psychology at the University of Chester, points to the growing number of people chatting to friends on social networks instead of actually meeting them. He had started on the assumption (*Annahme*) that friendships could be more efficiently maintained with the help of the social media. His findings indicate the contrary.

Against the background of more than 300 interviews, it has been revealed that people who do not use Facebook very often felt closer to their friends, were happier, and laughed more than those using social networks a lot.

What is interesting, too, was another revelation about active users and simple browsers of social networks in terms of the intensity of their friendships. Roberts found out that there is no difference between them. Personal contact cannot be replaced by any media, except by Skype, which made people similarly happy.

Follow-up activity

b) Have a look at the following box and then match the nouns with the respective topic:

Social networks: Twitter, Facebook, Linkedin, Pinterest, meetup, tumblr, instagram

Media: TV, newspapers, books, PCs

Telephones: cell phone, mobiles, landline phone, smart phone

Software programs: word, open office, linux

Surveillance: drones, CCTV, bugs, cameras, GPS

Search engines: google, lycos, bing, yahoo, yippy

Browser: firefox, opera, thunderbird, google, chrome

c) The following sentences in reported speech have to be transformed into direct speech:

1. Zuckerberg said that he had registered one billion users the month before.

Zuckerberg: I have registered one billion users last month.

2. Roberts asked what results would reveal new insights into friendship that would be published the following week.

Roberts asked: What results that will reveal new insights into friendship will be published next week?

3. Sandberg referred to Zuckerberg, saying that she had always been fond of him and that she was looking forward to working with him on new projects.

While talking about Zuckerberg she said: I have always been fond of him and I'm looking forward to working with him.

4. Gates said that he had spent billions on health care for African children and that he would even open another relief programme for sufferers of HIV.

Gates said: I have spent billions on health care for African children and I will even open another relief programme for sufferers of HIV.

d) Bennett has used some interesting, sometimes metaphorical expressions in her report. Make a list of them and state what they mean. Then select one you like and state why. There is an example at the beginning. After that select the one that you like best and say why.

quote	meaning	reference
friends click	friends do understand each other immediately	headline
they meet in the flesh	they meet in real life	headline, ll. 4 f.
who live their social lives online	who do not have real social contacts	l. 9
a way of staying in touch	keeping up/maintaining social contact	l. 15
who used text communications	not very sociable	l. 29
Skype came close to face-to-face contact	an almost personal contact, but not quite	l. 30

This is a matter of personal taste and choice. The first example above evokes the image of people matching in an ideal way.

The expressions 'who live their social lives online', is graphic and full of sarcasm, describing very poor genuine social relationships, maybe leading to what is, effectively, a form of isolation, a potentially dangerous situation reminding us of those murderers on a killing spree who had no other contacts but those on the web.

e) Imagine some friends of your 10-year-old brother want to fetch him for a football match, but he does not want to join them because he prefers to stay connected to Facebook at the moment. Against the background of the text, what would you tell him?

I don't think that this is a good idea. Would you really like me to tell them that you prefer that dumb PC to your friends? No way. You would lose them forever.

And I'll tell you what: those so-called "friends" on your social network are not friends at all. The whole thing is far too unrealistic compared to a real friendship. Just sitting in front of a PC is not the real thing for a boy. Football is far more than a game – it is kicking, laughing, joking – just real fun. And that is what makes a difference. Friendship has to be experienced every day face-to-face. Friends have to be in touch – in the literal sense of the word.

Acknowledgements

Images

p. 5: www.CartoonStock.com; p. 48: © Balint Radu – Fotolia.com; p. 49: Schöningh Verlagsarchiv

Every effort has been made to supply complete copyright information for the pictures included here. Should such entries be incomplete or contain errors, we request copyright owners to contact the publishers so that we can proceed with the necessary corrections.